BLACK MEN BUILT THE CAPITOL

*Discovering African-American History
In and Around Washington, D.C.*

JESSE J. HOLLAND

The
Globe
Pequot
Press

GUILFORD, CONNECTICUT

Copyright © 2007 Jesse Holland

Text design by Casey Shain
All photos by Jesse J. Holland except where otherwise noted
Some spot images courtesy www.photos.com

Library of Congress Cataloging-in-Publication Data is available.
978-0-7627-4536-4

Manufactured in the United States of America
First Edition/Seventh Printing

Contents

Minutes from the Maryland State Line
Harpers Ferry National Historical Park

Washington County
John Brown's Headquarters (Kennedy's Farm)

Annapolis
The Banneker-Douglass Museum
The Thurgood Marshall Memorial
Matthew Alexander Henson Memorial
The Kunta Kinte-Alex Haley Memorial

Baltimore County
Benjamin Banneker Historical Park and Museum

Baltimore
Billie Holiday Statue
Mother Mary Lange Monument, Oblate Sisters of Providence, and St. Francis Academy
Thurgood Marshall Memorial
Reginald F. Lewis Museum of Maryland African American History & Culture
National Great Blacks in Wax Museum
Frederick Douglass-Isaac Myers Maritime Park

Other Places of Interest
Harriet Tubman Sites
Frederick Douglass Birthplace Marker

Arlington
The Marine Corps War Memorial (Iwo Jima Memorial)
Women in Military Service for America Memorial
Arlington National Cemetery
The Custis Plantation
Freedman's Village

Mount Vernon
George Washington's Home
The Mount Vernon Slave Memorial
Slave Quarters at Mount Vernon

Alexandria
Alexandria Black History Museum
Alexandria African American Heritage Park

Petersburg
Petersburg National Battlefield Park

Preface

There's history in Washington, D.C. There has to be.

The District of Columbia can make a strong case that it is the most powerful city in the world. The most powerful man in the world lives at 1600 Pennsylvania Avenue NW, the nine top jurists in the country work out of the Supreme Court, and the greatest legislative body ever assemble daily in the United States Capitol.

With all of this existing within the space of only a few blocks, history is made daily in the District of Columbia. So why was it that when I looked for African-American history in the corridors of the powerful in the District of Columbia, I always felt disappointed?

Now, I want to be specific in what I'm talking about. Washington, D.C., is a "chocolate city." Everyone knows this. There are more African Americans here than any other race, and the city itself is filled with African-American history. And several books do a great job chronicling the African-American history of the District. (I recommend reading *A Guide to Black Washington: Places and Events of Interest in the Nation's Capital*; *The Black Washingtonians: The Anacostia Museum Illustrated Chronology*; and *The Hidden History of Washington, D.C.* if you're interested in the subject. They do a fabulous job of covering the District.)

But very few people come here to see the District. They come to see the White House, the National Mall, the Lincoln Memorial, the Jefferson Memorial, the Washington Monument, Arlington National Cemetery, the Smithsonian museums, and the U.S. Capitol. I know, because those are the places I wanted to see when I first came to Washington as a young student from Mississippi and again as a worldly working adult fresh out of upstate New York.

Millions of people who live here and visit here are just like me: We fill up the streets around the National Mall, the White House, and the U.S. Capitol drinking in the history of our government and the people who made it great.

But what if you're African American and want to know more about your people? What kind of history would you find if you just went to the places the rest of the tourists go: the National Mall, the White House, and the U.S. Capitol?

You'd find the same thing that I found: little or nothing.

But there's a history here. There has to be.

Despite its so-called air of international sophistication and its role as capital of the Union in the Civil War, Washington, D.C., is at heart a southern city. (It's even south of the Mason-Dixon Line!) And there is no part of the South that hasn't had a significant African-American presence for hundreds of years.

But why could I only find a couple of recent books on the subject at the local bookstores, and why are there only a couple of items on the walls of monuments and buildings here and there? We as African Americans have been here since the city was founded in 1790. Shouldn't there be some African-American history in those famous monuments and buildings? If you depended on what was available when I first came to Washington, you'd say no.

Even the politicians working in Washington seemed to realize how ridiculous the lack of information was. During the time I worked in the Capitol as a journalist from 2000 to 2007, they commissioned paintings of Senator Blanche Bruce and Representative Joseph Rainey, the first African-American senator and the first African-American representative, and placed a statue of Martin Luther King Jr. in the Capitol's Rotunda. President Clinton had his presidential portrait painted by an African-American artist. The Baltimore-Washington Airport was renamed after deceased Supreme Court Justice Thurgood Marshall. They even formed a committee to study the contributions of African-American slaves to the building of the Capitol, with a promise that a display might be put up in a new section of the building.

But despite how great all of those things were, I found myself saying, "Is that it?" Paintings and statues that most people will never see, and a promise of a display sometime in the future?

There's a history here. There has to be.

It was about this time when I first considered getting married. My future wife gave me a great birthday gift: a trip to a jazz festival in Virginia Beach, a stop at Busch Gardens, and a day at Colonial Williamsburg. It was there, at Colonial Williamsburg, that the idea for this book first started percolating in my head.

For those of you who don't know, Colonial Williamsburg is a living re-creation of what Williamsburg would have been like in colonial days, complete with reenactors dressed in colonial garb, restored buildings, shops, taverns, and so on. It's basically a big outdoor museum where people can go and see how Americans really lived during colonial days.

The day that my wife and I went, there was one tour posted on the schedule that really caught our eyes. It was called "How the Other Half Lived." I wish today that I could remember what our tour guide's name was because I would publicly thank him here. But since I can't remember his name, I'll just say that our guide, a large African-American man who was not dressed in period clothing (what exactly would he have been wearing if he were in Colonial Williamsburg at that time—rags?), took the small group of people that signed up for "How the Other Half Lived" and used an hour to tell a history of blacks at Colonial Williamsburg—a history that we had not learned or heard anything about in our previous hours in the park. As he told us, "The history you've learned here from everyone else is not incorrect; it's just incomplete if you don't include us."

A light went on in my head.

A year later my wedding day was approaching. I had spent the last year or so as a member of the Congressional Standing Committee of Correspondents (a group of reporters elected by other reporters to represent the media in front of Congress and regulate how the Capitol is covered). One of the responsibilities of this committee is deciding which reporters get credentials to cover Congress on a daily basis. So, whenever the Associated Press got a new reporter, they would send the person up to the Capitol so that I could shepherd him or her through the credentialing process. New reporters usually come from out of town, so in addition to getting them started in this process, I somehow ended up giving tours of the Capitol. And you know what? I started to like it!

But the more I did those quickie tours, the more it bothered me that there wasn't more information about African Americans in the Capitol. I know it's out there: African Americans around here have talked for years about the rumor that slaves built the Capitol and even erected the Statue of Freedom. A comic book that I bought—Marvel's "U.S. War Machine"—even has a reference to it! If Marvel knows it, why doesn't everybody else? I consider myself to be a reasonably intelligent human being, and I didn't know it to be a fact. Does anyone else?

I started doing some research of my own. With the assistance of the Architect of the Capitol, the Senate Historical Office, and the Library of Congress, as well as some good old Internet Web browser searching, I found out that it's not a rumor. It's true, and there are records to prove it.

My mind really began churning. If it's true about the Capitol, then what about the White House? I found that slaves helped build that, too. What about the National Mall? I found that slaves didn't participate in the building of any of the monuments (probably because most of them were built after the Civil War), but the National Mall sits right on the site of what was one of the city's most bustling slave markets and jails. Why doesn't everybody know this? Writers hear it all the time: Write what you would want to read.

My family came to the District for my wedding in 2004. We had a couple of hours to kill, so I piled them all into a rental van and gave them a quick tour of the city. With my wedding only hours away, I had to make it a short trip, so we headed down to the National Mall.

We visited the U.S. Capitol, the White House, the Lincoln Memorial, the Smithsonian museums, and the famous cherry-tree-lined Tidal Basin, but my mother wasn't impressed. You see, I'm the product of a long line of Mississippi teachers and farmers, a people who are fanatical about our family's history and African-American history. My folks still have the first acre of land that was purchased by my family after the Civil War. My brother is now refurbishing, modernizing, and moving into the house that my great-grandfather lived in, on land right down the road from the original family homestead. And I'm working on a genealogical database of my family that stretches back to when African Americans only had one name or took the name of the master's family.

On top of that, we're Mississippians. And being a Mississippian brings with it a certain obligation to know your history, good or bad, because someone's always going to ask. (One of the first questions I used to get when interviewing for a job outside of Mississippi was, "How could you stand living in Mississippi?" My routine answer was, "Have you ever *been* to Mississippi?" Their response was usually no. That's where I would sigh and begin extolling the virtues of the Magnolia State. It's not that I don't see the flaws, but home is where the heart is, right?)

D.C.'s national monuments were interesting, my mother said, but she wanted to see some of the city's famous African-American landmarks while she was here. "You already have," I said, smiling. "You just didn't know it. Did you know that black men built the Capitol?"

It took off from there. When it came time to write my first book, deciding that it would be *Black Men Built the Capitol* was an easy choice.

How did I know that it was time for me to write a book? You know that feeling you sometimes get that it's time to do something or you will never get it done? It's like a ticking clock in your head that says, "Either you get the ball rolling on this or give up hope that you'll ever get it done. Oh, and by the way, if you don't get something done, you're going to regret it for the rest of your life. And it'll be *all your fault!*" That's the feeling I'm talking about. I first got that feeling years ago while living in South Carolina, which set me down the road that eventually brought me to Washington.

I feel the need to say that I actually like living in the District of Columbia. Mississippi will always be home (all Mississippians are legally required to say that!), but Washington, D.C., holds a special place in my heart.

I bought my first house here (in Anacostia). I met my future wife here (in Capitol Hill), proposed to her here (at the Lincoln Memorial on the National Mall), and married her across the river (at historic Alfred Street Baptist Church in Alexandria, Virginia). The District of Columbia was also where I witnessed the birth of my daughter Rita (at Sibley Memorial Hospital in upper Northwest).

I've had one of the best jobs I've ever had in my life here, as a political reporter for the Associated Press in the U.S. Capitol and briefly at the White House. I don't have room to tell you about the people I've met, the places I've been, and the things I've done, but it's enough to say that I wouldn't have traded my time in Washington, D.C., for anything.

And then there's the city itself. Some of my fondest memories involve biking down to the Jefferson Memorial with my family to watch the Fourth of July fireworks explode over the National Mall from the Jefferson Memorial. Or strolling through Capitol Hill after the first snowfall, marveling at the beauty of the parks, circles, and houses with their sheer covering of white, fluffy snow. Or meandering down Independence Avenue after the cherry trees bloom, signaling the start of another gorgeous spring in the nation's capital.

In short, you could say I have a fairly strong emotional attachment to the District, especially for someone who has lived here less than a decade. So, whenever someone comes into the District to visit, I usually offer to give them a tour of the city and tell them something about Washington, D.C., and African Americans about whom they would never hear otherwise.

That's how *Black Men Built the Capitol* is organized—as if I were putting you in the back of my SUV, driving you around the District of Columbia, and explaining the African-American contributions to the city's greatest buildings and monuments. We start in the Capitol, the symbolic center of Washington, D.C., and one of the most majestic buildings in the city. From there we head west down Pennsylvania Avenue to the White House, the home of the president. Once we've finished there, we meander south toward the National Mall and its monuments and buildings.

For most tourists, and even for most Washingtonians, this is all they ever see of the District. And now, if this is all *you* want to see of Washington, D.C., when you finish these chapters you'll know more about African Americans and the District of Columbia than most nonhistorians.

But the stories don't end there. There's a history here. There has to be.

From here I want readers to follow me into the District of Columbia. I could have filled this book with notations of which famous African American lived here or which famous black bookstore was there, but I looked for places that have stories, places that have national significance, and places that people can actually visit and not just drive by. These are places I hope people might visit; I hope that they might pull this book out of their back pocket, read the section written about whatever they're looking at, and say, "You know what? I'm glad I now know that."

And let me tell you another secret about Washington, D.C. It wouldn't exist without Maryland and Virginia. The District was carved out of Maryland and Virginia, and it's rare for a person to come to Washington, D.C., without visiting either our southern or our northern neighbor. Given how closely things are squeezed together in the District, my family often drives over to either Maryland or Virginia for a bite to eat, a quick vacation (Assateague Island in Maryland or Virginia Beach in Virginia are our favorites), or to go the local shopping malls.

Since Maryland and Virginia have such a close relationship to the District, I felt that I should include some of the important African-American sites in those states. There are other books you can find that explain African-American history in Maryland and Virginia in more detail, but I've included some of the top places I think you shouldn't pass by when you come to the District. I've tried not to include anything that would take more than a couple of hours to get to, and I've organized the book so you won't miss anything if you're heading down to the beach or to an amusement park.

One more thing: I've had many people ask whether I'm writing a history book or a travel book. My hope is that you'll consider this a history book that travels well. I was purposefully trying not to write a scholarly history book that would end up sitting on someone's dusty shelves, never to be opened.

I mentioned earlier that I come from a family of teachers. My mother and father are retired teachers, my grandparents were teachers, my uncles and aunts are teachers, my cousins are teachers, and even my youngest brother is a teacher. Given the fact that I've lived around teachers for so long, I can say for a fact that even teachers don't carry their history books out the front door with them when they go someplace. I want people to carry this book with them when they go out into Washington, D.C., because I can almost guarantee you that the information in this book will not be shared with you by any of the official tour guides you might meet in the District. I'm not saying that you should not to listen to them; I'm saying what the Colonial Williamsburg tour guide said to me: "The history you've learned here from everyone else is not incorrect; it's just incomplete if you don't include us."

One thing I do have to be up front with you about before I let you wander through the African-American history of our nation's capital is the fact that this book is not complete. In fact, it's far from being complete. There will be future editions that will feature all new African-American attractions in Washington, D.C. How can I be sure of this? Well, the final chapter of this book is called "On the Verge of a True Black Renaissance," and it includes soon-to-be-opened museums and memorials like the Martin Luther King Jr. National Monument on the National Mall, the Smithsonian Institution National Museum of African American History and Culture, and the National Slavery Museum in Fredericksburg, Virginia.

On top of that, Congress has announced plans to include statues inside the U.S. Capitol of Rosa Parks, the mother of the Civil Rights movement, and Sojourner Truth, one of the leading African-American female speakers of her time. There's a great story about Sojourner Truth in the White House chapter. I can't wait to move that story into the Capitol chapter once her statue is erected.

When all of these monuments and museums are open to the public, no trip to Washington, D.C., will be complete without including them.

Every day, every week, every month, every year, we Americans find out completely new things about the history of African Americans in this country and in this city. Hopefully there will always be people willing to share with the general public the things they find out. I know I'm going to keep digging.

Now turn the page and begin exploring Washington, D.C. There's history here.

Enjoy!

Jesse J. Holland

P.S. My mother told me when I was young that you have to be responsible for your own actions and the consequences that follow. Therefore, the credit for any success this book achieves goes to all of those who helped me along the way. Any mistakes that were made are solely my responsibility.

Now that I've said that, if there's anything you want to say about *Black Men Built the Capitol* (whether you liked it, didn't like it, want to see more, or have something you think should be added to future editions) feel free to e-mail me at jesse@jessejholland.com.

Acknowledgments

First and foremost I thank the two loves of my life, Carol June and Rita Elaine. Without them none of this would have been possible. This book is dedicated to them.

I also want to thank my parents, Jesse and Yvonne, who taught me that anything is possible if you're willing to take a chance and work for it; my siblings, Twyla, Candace, and Fred, who keep me grounded and humble; my nieces, Alexandria and Samantha, who taught me joy; my best friends, Lee Eric, Amy, and Rodney, who taught me that you can dream about the stars and still keep your feet firmly here on the ground; my frats, who kept me sane for the longest time: Mark Stephens in Carolina and Chandler Mouton and the rest of the Brothers of the Eta Zeta chapter of Omega Psi Phi at Ole Miss; my in-laws, Rita Joy, Mark, Leslie, and Soreya; Dr. Will Norton, formerly of the University of Mississippi and now of the University of Nebraska-Lincoln, the first person who truly made me believe that I could write; David and Lain, my HATBaG buddies, for introducing truly creative writing into my life; Shannon, Joe, Tutor, Baker, Goodwin, Rushing, and everyone else at *The Daily Mississippian* for some of the most entertaining nights of my life; Dr. Samir Husni and the rest of the journalism professors at the University of Mississippi, who kept me in line while I was working at the *Mississippian;* Eve, Mona, Pete, Bob, Jack, Colette, Christie, Nikki, Carrie, Dave, Leigh, Bill, John, Jim, Jennifer, and the rest of the South Carolina crew for being there when I needed friends in a new place; Robert Naylor, Mark Humbert, and everybody at AP–Albany who taught me to love the snow; Sandy Johnson and everybody at AP–Washington, for being patient with me as I worked my way through this book and back to the real world; and finally, to all my friends and relatives who were there for me along the way: all my aunts and uncles, but especially Joyce; all my cousins, but especially Renita, Casey, Stacey, San, Sean, and Tiffany; all of the teachers, professors, and instructors at H. W. Byers High School and the University of Mississippi; Sonya, Darlene, Janelle, Mike Woolfolk, and Kymm Hunter; Ralph Eubanks for hooking me up with the people who brought you this book; the librarians at the Washington, D.C., public library system, the Alexandria public library system, and the Library of Congress; the researchers at the National Archives, Barbara Wolanin, and the ladies in the Capitol Curator's office; William Allen, Richard Baker, and everyone who took the time to help me craft this book. There are hundreds of more people I could mention here (and they know who they are), but I want to end with heartfelt thanks to you, the reader. Thanks for taking a chance on this book. I hope you enjoy it.

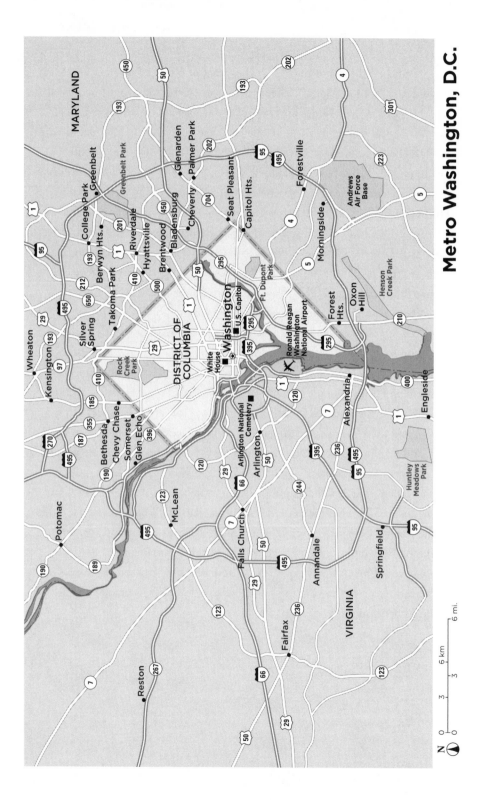

Metro Washington, D.C.

The UNITED STATES CAPITOL

What Everyone Already Knows

The U.S. Capitol is one of the most recognizable buildings in existence, the home of one of the most powerful branches of the U.S. government, and one of the world's best-known symbols of liberty. Millions of people see videos, photos, or illustrations of the Capitol's majestic and grandiose white dome every day, while millions of others come to Washington, D.C., to see the building in person or to observe the legislative branch of the American government in action.

In addition to being the home of Congress, the Capitol is the location for historically important ceremonies such as presidential inaugurations, speeches by foreign leaders, and state funerals. The Capitol is also a world-class American history and art museum for those interested in learning more about this nation's past.

The Capitol was always intended to be the centerpiece of the new "Federal City," as can be seen in the plans of French designer Pierre L'Enfant. L'Enfant decided to locate the "Congress House" on top of what was then known as Jenkins Hill, and he designed Washington, D.C., around it, having broad avenues named after the original thirteen states radiating from the building. While it is no longer the geographical center of the city, as it was when the "Federal City" was first envisioned, the Capitol is still considered the symbolic heart of Washington, D.C., and the nation as a whole.

President George Washington had a hand in selecting the building's design, choosing Dr. William Thorton's plans for the new home for the Senate, the

Photograph of African-American soldiers drilling in front of the East Front of the U.S. Capitol   LIBRARY OF CONGRESS, LCUSA729 9929

House of Representatives, and the Supreme Court during a design competition. Washington laid the cornerstone for the building in 1793, and construction began. Congress would not wait for the building's completion to occupy it, however. Congress met in the incomplete building on November 17, 1800.

The road to completion was long, with the work on the new Capitol being halted when invading British soldiers burned the still-unfinished Capitol during the War of 1812. A second work stoppage occurred during the Civil War, when the building was used as a military barracks and hospital for Union forces. Only after the Civil War would the construction of the Capitol be considered finished with the completion of the world-famous dome and the topping of the building with the now-famous Statue of Freedom.

Black Men Built the Capitol

While millions of people tour the Capitol every year, few know or are told about the contributions that blacks made to the heart and soul of the U.S. government— no minor oversight. The Capitol would not exist as we know it today without slave craftsmanship and labor.

Records show that slaves who lived in the Washington, D.C., area made up a good portion of the labor pool that worked on the Capitol. More than four hundred slaves, or more than half of the documented workforce that constructed the Capitol, cleared trees from Jenkins Hill and dug up stumps for the wide avenues that radiate out into the city, according to research first publicized by NBC reporter Edward Hotaling in 2000. We now know that slaves baked the bricks used for the building's foundation and walls, sawed lumber for the interior walls and floors, dug the trenches for the foundation, worked the Virginia quarries where the sandstone was cut, and laid the stones that hold up the Capitol to this day. "In rebuilding the Capitol, the White House, and other public structures destroyed by the British in 1814, gangs of hired slaves did the bulk of the work," wrote Constance McLaughlin Green in her 1967 book *The Secret City: A History of Race Relations in the Nation's Capital.*

Many of the slaves were likely hired from Virginia, Maryland, and District of Columbia farms and households. The largest slaveholding state in America was Virginia, with a little more than 400,000 slaves living there before the Civil War. People in the District of Columbia and Maryland also had their share of slaves, with as many as 3,185 slaves residing in the federal capital and another 100,000 living in Maryland.

Slaves wearing handcuffs and shackles passing the U.S. Capitol, ca. 1815
LIBRARY OF CONGRESS, LC-USZ62-2574

The construction of the Capitol and other federal buildings in Washington was a windfall for slave owners, with "public records attesting to the fact that the $5-per-month payment for that African-American slave labor was made directly to slave owners and not to the laborer," according to congressional legislation introduced in 2000 to study the use of slave labor in the Capitol's construction. Slave owner Edmund Plowden, who lived in what is now St. Mary's County, Maryland, owned sixty-four slaves and rented out three men—Gerard, Tony, and Jack—to work at the Capitol. Although Plowden did not lift a single stone or cut down a single tree, he made $15 a month off of the Capitol construction. He was only required to provide his slaves with a blanket.

The use of slave labor benefited the government as well as slave owners. If white workers demanded higher salaries, the government could threaten to replace them with cheap slave labor.

Little is known about the slaves themselves other than some of their names and the fact that they lived in ramshackle huts around the Capitol along with white paid laborers. Although they received no money for their regular work, the slaves did get rations and medical care while working on the Capitol, with some likely getting more than they would have gotten if they had been working on the local farms.

Slaves were sometimes paid if they worked more than their masters required (for example, if they worked on Sunday in addition to the normal Monday through Saturday workweek). One slave named Peter received one pound for making a coffin for "public negroes."

Of the existing Capitol facade, only the west elevation of the old north wing (the only part not covered by later additions) can be directly attributed to slave labor. The Virginia sandstone quarried by slaves can still be seen.

Route to Freedom?

Building the Capitol for little or no pay was certainly not a good time. Slaves likely made attempts to flee to the North while working on the Capitol. There was at least one escape attempt by a slave named Jacob, who made his break for freedom on a broken leg by leaving the group that was digging the foundation of the Capitol at the beginning of September 1793. It is not known whether he made it.

Philip Reid and the Statue of Freedom

Blacks were not just brute labor at the Capitol. They also brought highly special-
ized expertise in carpentry, bricklaying, ironworking, and other skilled trades, as
the Statue of Freedom on top of the Capitol dome shows.

When the Capitol was first constructed, the building had a small wood-and-
copper dome with none of the grandeur of the current dome. It was considered a
national embarrassment. The responsibility for coming up with a new dome was
given to architect and designers Thomas U. Walter and Montgomery Meigs, who
designed and constructed the current white cast-iron dome that we see today.

Two months after Congress authorized the construction of the new Capitol
dome in 1855, sculptor Thomas Crawford was given a commission to create a
statue that would sit on top of the new structure. Crawford was a white man
who had a couple of run-ins with slave owner and future president of the Confederacy Jefferson Davis because of Crawford's desire to make the statue one of a
freed slave. Crawford completed a nineteen-foot, six-inch plaster model of Freedom in 1856 while living in Rome. (According to the Architect of the Capitol,
Crawford wanted to top the statue with a liberty cap, the symbol of freed slaves
in ancient Greece. Davis, in his capacity as U.S. war secretary, objected to this
idea, saying in a January 15, 1856, letter that "its history renders it inappropriate
to a people who were born free and would not be enslaved." Crawford relented,
replacing the liberty cap with a crested Roman helmet. He would die the next
year in London without ever seeing his work atop the Capitol.)

If not for the ingenuity of Philip Reid, a slave of mixed blood, the story of
the Freedom statue would end with the plaster model arriving in America and
sitting on the grounds of the Capitol. Reid, a thirty-nine-year-old slave from
Charleston, South Carolina, was owned by ironworker Clark Mills, who
described Reid as a "highly-esteemed" workman who was "smart in mind" and
"a good workman in a foundry." Reid came up with Mills to Washington, D.C.,
from South Carolina, where the slave had worked in a foundry for his entire life.
Mills noted in an 1863 document that he bought Reid "because of his evident
talent for the foundry business." Reid proved his intelligence and skill in two
different incidents involving the Statue of Freedom.

Solving the Mystery of the Plaster Model. Once the plaster model of the
Statue of Freedom made it to the Capitol grounds, an Italian workman assembled

it near the building so everyone could see what Freedom would look like when it was finished and on top of the dome.

Author S. D. Wyeth described what happened next in his 1869 book *The Federal City: Ins and Abouts of Washington:*

> The Italian was ordered to take the model apart. This he positively refused to do, unless he was given a large increase of wages, and secured employment for a number of years. He said, he alone "knew how to separate it," and would do so only upon such conditions.

This Italian worker thought he was the only person in the country skilled enough to take apart the plaster model without injuring it, but Philip Reid proved him wrong.

Wyeth continued:

> His plan of working was this: A pulley and tackle were brought into use, and its hook inserted into an iron eye affixed to the head of the figure. The rope was then gently strained repeatedly until the uppermost joining of the top section of the model began to make a faint appearance. This gave some indication as to the whereabouts of its bolts inside, and led to their discovery; and thus, finally, one after another of the sections was discovered, their bolts unloosed, and the model, uninjured, made ready for the foundry.

Who knows what the government might have decided to do with Freedom if Reid had not figured out how to get the pieces apart without giving in to the Italian craftsman's demands. Would they have cancelled the entire project? Would they have left the plaster model on the Capitol grounds and placed another statue on the dome? Or might another craftsman have damaged the plaster model in a futile attempt to separate the sections, making it impossible for Freedom to ever be cast in bronze? Thankfully, because of Philip Reid, we never had to find out.

A Black Master Builder at the Foundry. The story of Philip Reid and the Statue of Freedom doesn't end there. There is a second account of Freedom and a slave, also believed to be Reid, who put even more of an African-American stamp on the statue.

Clark Mills was paid $400 a month by the federal government to cast Freedom in bronze at his foundry. But another dispute over money interrupted the work. On December 10, 1863, the *New York Tribune* described the situation:

A Tribute to Philip Reid

The only information available on what happened to Reid after slaves in the District of Columbia were freed indicates that he stayed in the Washington, D.C., area and opened a shop. S. D. Wyeth wrote, "Mr. Reid, the former slave, is now in business for himself, and highly esteemed by all who know him." There are no monuments or plaques or paintings of Reid, so we don't know what he looked like. But the federal government did keep the plaster model of Freedom that it took Reid's genius to get apart. It is located today in the basement of the Russell Senate Office Building, a silent monument to Reid's skill.

Congressional officials plan to move the plaster model of the Statue of Freedom to a more visible spot in the Congressional Visitor Center when it opens in 2008. Congressional officials also are considering putting up some kind of memorial to the slave workers who helped construct the Capitol, perhaps also in the visitor center.

When the bronze castings were being completed, in a foundry of Mr. Mills, near Bladensburg, his fireman, who had superintended the work from the beginning, and who was receiving $8 per day, struck and demanded $10, assuring Mr. M that the advance must be granted to him, as nobody in America, except himself, could complete the work. Mr. M felt that the demand was exorbitant, and appealed in his dilemma to the slaves who were assisting in the molding. "I can do that well," said one of them, an intelligent and ingenious servant who had been intimately engaged in the various processes. The striker was dismissed, and the negro, assisted occasionally by the finer skill of his master, took the striker's place as superintendent, and the work went on. The black master-builder lifted the ponderous uncouth masses, and bolted them together, joint to joint, piece by piece, till they blended into the majestic "Freedom" who to-day lifts her head in the blue clouds above Washington, invoking a benediction on this imperiled Republic!

The slave is never named in the *New York Tribune* story, but it is likely, given the description of the slave's skill, that it was Reid. Thus, it took a slave to get work started on Freedom (by figuring out how to take the plaster model apart), and it took a black man to supervise the creation of the statue that sits atop the Capitol.

Few history books mention Reid or the work he did, but his service is well documented in congressional records. In an address to Congress in 1928 (as preserved in the Congressional Record), one of the statue's most reverent supporters, William Cox, said that the successful dismantling and handling of the model:

> was due to the faithful service and genius of an intelligent negro in Washington named Philip Reid, a mulatto slave owned by Mr. Clark Mills, and that much credit is due him for his faithful and intelligent services rendered in modeling and casting America's superb Statue of Freedom, which kisses the first rays of the aurora of the rising sun as they appear upon the apex of the Capitol's wonderful dome.

Reid's skill was such that he was one of the few slaves paid personally *in addition* to his master being compensated for his time and labor. In 1861 the

The Capitol

The 535 members of the Senate and the House of Representatives who work in the Capitol are the only popularly elected members of the American government, and therefore they are the ones most

directly accountable to the people. (The leader of the executive branch, the president, is elected for a maximum of two four-year terms through an electoral system, while members of the judicial branch, the Supreme Court, are selected in conjunction by the executive and legislative branches. The 100 senators are directly elected to six-year terms, and the 435 House members serve two-year terms.) The Senate works in the building's north wing, while House members legislate from the wing south of the Rotunda, an ornate and world-renowned room in the center of the Capitol.

The majority of the Capitol is open only for invited guests or official state business, although guided tours of the public portions are offered on a daily basis. The offices of the senators and representatives also offer official tours of the building and surrounding grounds upon request.

federal government paid Reid $1.25 a Sunday for "keeping up fires under the moulds," according to a pay stub found in the government records. At the bottom of the sheet is Reid's "X," which is how people who could not read signed documents.

The African-American Presence in the Capitol

Statuary Hall

The contributions of African Americans didn't end with the construction of the walls and statues of the Capitol. Historical records show that slaves also are responsible for some of the most impressive architectural features inside the Capitol. Some of these contributions are on display in Statuary Hall, the home of many of the statues donated by the fifty states to honor their greatest citizens, and the original chamber of the House of Representatives.

Congress was anxious to restore amphitheatre-shaped Statuary Hall—the site of several presidential inaugurations—to its previous glory after British troops burned the Capitol during the War of 1812. To that end, the federal government contracted with a man named John Hartnet to provide the colossal columns of variegated breccia marble to stand along the walls of House and Senate chambers. This marble was to be quarried from Noland's Ferry, Maryland, which was located along the Potomac River in an area that is now known as northern Montgomery County. But Hartnet proved to be a poor choice because he was "woefully unprepared," according to William Allen, the architectural historian for the Architect of the Capitol, who has written several books on the building's architecture and art.

Hartnet failed to quarry, cut, and polish the marble from Noland's Ferry at the speed needed to complete the reconstruction of the House and Senate chambers, so the federal government decided to hire workers to complete the project. Many of the workers were slaves from nearby farms. While the government did not pay these slaves for their work, it provided clothing and temporary housing for them as they successfully quarried, cut, and polished the marble column shafts and sent them up the Potomac to Washington for placement. Those same marble shafts can now be seen along the walls of Statuary Hall and the old Senate chamber, one of the few places in the Capitol where tourists can still touch something historians and academics can positively attest was worked on by slaves.

As a "reward" for their work, the slaves were to be returned to enslavement in the fields and farms from which they were brought. Meanwhile, their masters received payment from the federal government.

The only way to gain admission to Statuary Hall is to take a guided tour. As the tour guide tells you about the presidents who served in Statuary Hall and the weird acoustics that prompted representatives to leave the room for their current chamber, wander over to one of the walls and place your hand on one of the marble shafts. When you do, think about how much of the Capitol was crafted by slaves and how much work they put into a building that meant freedom to everyone in the world except themselves.

The Rotunda

The Rotunda is the symbolic and figurative heart of the U.S. Capitol and the most awe-inspiring room visitors will encounter in the Washington, D.C., area. With its magnificent view of the interior of the Capitol dome and wondrous paintings and statues, it is one of the grandest and most historically important places in Washington, D.C. Tour guides bring thousands of people through the Rotunda daily and explain in detail the historical meanings behind the life-size artwork on the circular walls and the interior of the dome, which was meant in its day to record the history of the young nation. Not a single painting in the room

Rosa Parks

Rosa Parks is credited with having sparked the civil rights movement by refusing to give up her seat on a Montgomery, Alabama, city bus. Parks, who was working as a seamstress, refused to move  on December 1, 1955, when a bus driver demanded that she and three other patrons give up their seats so a white man could sit. The other three people moved. Rosa Parks was arrested, and four days later she was found guilty of disorderly conduct. Her decision led to the now-famous Montgomery bus boycott and the rising national prominence of a young black minister named Martin Luther King Jr.

depicts a black—an irony in a building that was constructed with the sweat and labor of slaves.

The Rotunda, however, houses the only statue in the Capitol dedicated to an African American: a bust of civil rights leader Martin Luther King Jr. Added to the Capitol collection in 1986, four days before the first national celebration of the federal Martin Luther King Jr. holiday, the bronze bust of a youthful King is one and a half times life-size and rests on a 5½-foot black pedestal.

On December 21, 1982, Congress passed a resolution calling for the statue. The bust was intended "to serve to memorialize [Dr. King's] contributions on such matters as the historic legislation of the 1960s affecting civil rights and the right to vote." African-American sculptor John Wilson beat 180 other sculptors in a competition and received a $50,000 congressional commission to complete the work of King wearing a coat and tie and a pensive, somber expression. The bust was unveiled on January 16, 1986, which would have been King's fifty-seventh birthday. The bust serves as a permanent reminder "of our moral obligation to civil rights," Coretta Scott King said at the unveiling of the bust in a 1986 Rotunda ceremony.

The Rotunda is also used to honor some of America's greatest citizens after their death through a procedure called "lying in state," "lying in honor," or "lying in repose." It is a tradition in which a person's coffin is placed in the exact center of the Rotunda, where mourners can come and pay respect to the deceased. To have one's remains presented to the public inside the Capitol is considered a great honor. It is allowed only with a congressional resolution or permission from the congressional leadership. The family of the deceased must also grant permission. Only presidents and former military officials can lie in state. All others are considered to be lying in honor or in repose, terms that can be used interchangeably.

Since July 1, 1852, thirty-two people have been honored by having their remains presented to the public in the Rotunda, including eleven presidents. That list includes only one woman, an African-American woman: Rosa Parks.

After years of adoration as the "Mother of the Civil Rights Movement," Rosa Parks died October 24, 2005. Congress moved swiftly, passing Senate Concurrent Resolution 61 a few days later, stating, "in recognition of the historic contributions of Rosa Parks, her remains be permitted to lie in honor in the rotunda of the Capitol from October 30 to October 31, 2005, so that the citizens

Martin Luther King Jr. *by John Wilson*

of the United States may pay their last respects to this great American." Parks's casket was delivered to the Capitol by motorcade, led by the hearse and a vintage Washington, D.C., city bus. Her remains were carried up the West Front steps of the Capitol into the Rotunda by a military honor guard as thousands of people waited for their chance to pay their respects.

An estimated fifty thousand people paid their respects that day, including President George W. Bush, the Senate and House leadership, and future Supreme Court Justice Samuel Alito, and the event was broadcast internationally. Senate Chaplain Barry Black, the first African American to ever serve in that position, said Rosa Parks's courage "ignited a movement that aroused our national conscience" and served as an example of the "power of fateful, small acts."

The *first* African American to be honored with a ceremonial viewing in the Capitol Rotunda was Jacob Joseph Chestnut, a U.S. Capitol policeman who was killed while working at the building on July 24, 1998. On that day, an armed gunman attempted to enter the Capitol through the Memorial Doors on the first floor of the East Front, and Chestnut was fatally shot in his attempt to stop him. The gunman fatally shot a second Capitol policeman, Detective John Gibson, in the office of Majority Whip Tom DeLay (R-TX), before being stopped. The future Senate majority leader, Senator Bill Frist (R-TN), a heart surgeon, arrived soon after the shootings and attempted to help Chestnut, but both officers died later that day in area hospitals.

The two officers were honored by having their remains lie in repose in the Capitol Rotunda. They were also recognized at a memorial held in their honor in the Rotunda, which included speakers such as President Bill Clinton, Vice

Honoring Officer J. J. Chestnut

"So many times upon entering this building, I've been greeted by Officer Chestnut standing proudly at his post," Vice President Al Gore said in a memorial to the two officers who were killed. Bill Clinton, who laid a wreath for the two men, added: "Officer J. J. Chestnut and Detective John Gibson loved justice. The story of what they did here on Friday in the line of duty is already a legend."

President Al Gore, House Speaker Newt Gingrich (R-GA), and Senate Majority Leader Trent Lott (R-MS).

Chestnut, a twenty-year veteran of the Air Force, is one of many African Americans now buried in Arlington National Cemetery. In addition, he also is the only African American memorialized in a plaque in the U.S. Capitol: the Chestnut-Gibson plaque at the Memorial Door on the first floor of the Capitol.

The Senate

One of the greatest thrills of visiting the Capitol is watching Congress at work, and hundreds of people line up every day for a chance to enter the Senate chamber and watch members of the "Upper House" debate the issues of the day. Visitors are only allowed to enter the Senate chamber through designated third-floor entrances, which are guarded by Capitol police. However, while waiting to get inside the chamber, take a moment to look at the representations of African Americans in the art outside the Senate chamber—this art in itself will tell you a story.

Portrait of Senator Blanche K. Bruce. The most prominent depiction of an African American is a portrait of Senator Blanche K. Bruce of Mississippi, the first African American to serve a full term in the U.S. Senate. Located across from the Senate gallery doors nearest to the East Staircase, the oil-on-canvas painting of Bruce was commissioned by the Senate Commission on Art in 1999 and unveiled in the Capitol in 2001. Painted by African-American artist Simmie Knox, who also painted President Bill Clinton's portrait for the White House's art collection, the portrait is based on one of the few historical photographs of Bruce known to exist.

Elected to the U.S. Senate by the Mississippi state legislature during Reconstruction in 1874, Bruce served only one term, but during that time he became the first African American to preside over the Senate. A former slave who had escaped to freedom from Virginia, Bruce moved to Mississippi, bought a cotton plantation, and became rich through real estate before being sent to the Senate.

His wealth did not help him gain acceptance from all of his colleagues, however. James Alcorn, the other senator from Mississippi, refused to accompany Bruce as he headed to the front of the chamber to take his official oath of office on his first day. Bruce started down the aisle alone, but midway a New

Senator Blanche Kelso Bruce by Simmie Lee Knox   U.S. SENATE COLLECTION

York senator, Roscoe Conklins, joined him and walked with him to the front of the room.

The end of Reconstruction denied Bruce a second term when his first one ended in 1881, as southern states began to enact Jim Crow–style laws. Bruce worked several other government jobs and posts—including two tenures as register of the treasury, where he was the first African American with his signature on U.S. currency—until his death in 1898. The Senate would not have another African-American senator until Edward Brooke in 1967.

Reconstruction and Congress

After the Civil War, Congress passed the Thirteenth, Fourteenth, and Fifteenth Amendments to the Constitution (abolishing slavery; automatically

MORE FACTS making everyone born or naturalized inside the United States a citizen; and forbidding the use of race, color, or former condition of servitude as a barrier to voting). Republicans also took over and ran the governments of the defeated Southern states, enfranchising thousands of African Americans who had not previously been allowed to vote. But by 1877 the northern Republicans had agreed to return power to the southern Democrats. Southerners in turn immediately started restricting the rights of African Americans to vote; they imposed literacy tests, poll taxes, and white primaries, and they used intimidation tactics to deter African Americans. The last African-American senator from the South was Blanche Bruce of Mississippi, who was elected in 1874. The last black southern representative elected from the South was George Henry White of North Carolina, elected in 1897. There were no African Americans in Congress for the next twenty-eight years and none from the South until Barbara Jordan of Texas and Andrew Young of Georgia in 1973.

Hannibal Collins and The Battle of Lake Erie. A second painting with a representation of an African American is on the third floor. *The Battle of Lake Erie* by William Henry Powell, also an oil-on-canvas painting, sits above the Senate's east staircase. In the painting, Master Commandant Oliver Hazard Perry is abandoning his sinking flagship, the *Lawrence,* to continue the battle aboard another ship in his fleet. Perry and his sailors eventually captured the six-ship British fleet, a major victory in the War of 1812, which sparked the famous message from Perry to his superiors: "We have met the enemy and they are ours."

In Powell's painting, six oarsmen are rowing Perry over to another ship, the *Niagara,* where he would lead his fleet to victory. One of those oarsmen is a black. Henry Tuckerman identified the man in his 1867 *Book of the Artists* as

"Perry's black servant Hannibal," who responds to a near-hit in "evident consternation."

The man's face could belong to one of the slave workers at the Capitol,
since Powell used workers in the building as his models for the painting. The
man himself may not have been Perry's servant, however. Several historians say
that the sailor could be Hannibal Collins, a freed slave from Newport, Rhode
Island, who fought with the First Rhode Island Regiment during the Revolutionary War. Records show that Collins was injured during the Battle of Rhode
Island but enlisted again during the War of 1812 under Perry and fought at the
Battle of Lake Erie. The Newport, Rhode Island, Historical Society also says
Collins was on the boat that took Perry to the *Niagara* when he transferred his
flag at the crucial point in the battle; this would make Powell's representation in
the Senate painting historically accurate. Collins survived the battle and went on
to serve with Perry in South America.

Crispus Attucks and the Boston Massacre. The two other paintings
depicting African Americans on the Senate side are on the Capitol's first floor,
and both are connected to the great Italian artist Constantino Brumidi.

Brumidi, who painted the famous *The Apotheosis of Washington* in the inte-
rior of the Capitol dome and the extensive frescoes and murals in the Brumidi
Corridors, is also responsible for the artwork inside the historical Senate
Appropriation Committee rooms. On the north wall of S-128 sits Brumidi's
interpretation of the Boston Massacre. In the exact center of that painting is
Crispus Attucks, the first black to be killed for the United States. Attucks is
often portrayed as being one of the leaders arguing against the presence of
British troops. He is often depicted holding a club, as he is in Brumidi's decoration. British troops fired into the protesters, immediately killing Attucks and
four white men.

Many consider the Boston Massacre to be the incident that sparked the
Revolutionary War, and Attucks to be one of the first martyrs for American free-
dom. This fresco is the earliest representation of an African American in the
Capitol.

Dr. Ronald McNair and the Challenger Astronauts. The most recent
painting depicting an African American on the Senate side honors some of the
United States' fallen heroes in a space that Brumidi left vacant in the Senate

corridors on the first floor. Brumidi painted a series of ornate murals in the hall-ways of the Capitol, with scenes representing American history, culture, people, animals, and plants in what are now called the Brumidi Corridors. However, Brumidi never finished the work, and several ovals and diamonds were left blank. So far the Senate has commissioned artists to fill two of those spaces with depictions of events that are deemed to be of national importance.

The explosion of the space shuttle *Challenger* in January 1986, which killed all seven astronauts aboard, is the subject of one of the new paintings. One of those astronauts was Dr. Ronald McNair, a *Challenger* team member and one of the first African-American astronauts in space. McNair is depicted in the mural holding his helmet and wearing his flight suit, along with his six shipmates. Several schools and awards have been named after McNair since his death.

The House

African Americans are also represented in artwork in several places in the House of Representatives' wing of the Capitol. The most prominent painting is that of Representative Joseph Rainey, a South Carolina Republican who in 1870 became the first African American to serve in the House of Representatives.

Portrait of Rep. Joseph Rainey. Painted by Simmie Knox, Rainey's painting is located on "Minority Row" outside the main bank of elevators near the House Radio/TV Gallery. Hanging with Rainey's painting are the portraits of the first female and the first Hispanic House members: Jeannette Rankin and Romualdo Pacheco. Rainey predated both of them, serving five terms in the House starting in 1870, before the end of Reconstruction allowed South Carolina to institute discriminatory laws that made it impossible for him to be reelected.

Rainey was born a slave, but his father bought his entire family's freedom in Georgetown, South Carolina, and taught him a barber's trade. During the Civil War, he was forced to work on the fortifications in the harbor of Charleston, South Carolina, but he managed to escape to the West Indies where he waited out the war.

Returning to South Carolina after the Confederacy's defeat, he briefly served as a state-level politician before being elected to Congress. In 1874 Rainey became the first African American to preside over the House. After leaving the House, Rainey worked as an internal revenue officer for South Carolina for several years before returning to private life in the banking and brokerage business in Washington, D.C. He died in Georgetown, South Carolina, in 1887.

An African-American Boy in Westward the Course of Empire Takes Its Way.

At the top of the House's west stairway, *Westward the Course of Empire Takes Its Way* includes a depiction of an African American. The mural was painted by Emanuel Leutze, a German-born American artist who is best known for his painting of Gen. George Washington crossing the Delaware during the Revolutionary War. In 1860 Congress commissioned Leutze to paint a mural for the Capitol, and *Westward the Course of Empire Takes Its Way* was the result.

Leutze completed his romanticized depiction of American settlers heading west in 1861, as the Civil War was raging between the North and the South. The oil-on-canvas picture has everything: frontiersmen, cowboys, farmers, and musicians. It even depicts a Madonna-like woman and child, and holding their donkey in the center of the painting is an African-American boy. The boy is stroking the muzzle of the donkey as he leads it toward what is obviously meant to be the promised land, as the United States is fighting a war to free African Americans from slavery.

The African-American boy is not in the original oil study of *Westward*. Leutze added the figure while completing the painting in the Capitol in 1862. Although no one knows why the boy was added, it is reasonable to assume that the artist's addition of an African American was in response to the Civil War and President Lincoln's decision to sign the Emancipation Proclamation that year.

An African-American Boy in Cornwallis Sues for Cessation of Hostilities under the Flag of Truce, 1857.

The only one of these paintings and frescoes ever displayed inside a congressional chamber, *Cornwallis Sues for Cessation of Hostilities under the Flag of Truce, 1857* is another of Italian artist Constantino Brumidi's works and was originally prominently featured in the southwest corner of the House chamber.

This fresco depicts Gen. George Washington and his staff in Yorktown talking to an emissary of Lord Cornwallis, who is accompanied by a drummer boy carrying a flag of truce. The British boy is not the only youth in the fresco, however. On the right side of the painting, the last figure in the scene is an African-American boy clearly wearing civilian garb.

Little information about this boy is available. One could assume that he is one of Washington's many slaves, or perhaps a freedman fighting for the Revolutionary Army. Either way, this fresco stayed in the House chamber from 1857 until 1950, when it was covered during the remodeling of the House chamber. Then, in 1961, it was cut out of the wall and moved to the House dining room, suffering extensive damage during the trip. In 1989 the fresco was professionally restored and can still be seen in the House dining room.

African Americans in the First-Floor House Corridors. African Americans most frequently appear in Capitol art in the Cox Corridors, the House's equivalent of the Senate's Brumidi Corridors. In 1952, artist Allyn Cox was hired to complete the panoramic frieze in the Rotunda, which had been left incomplete by Brumidi's death. As the result of his success, in 1973 Cox was given the responsibility of painting the ceilings of the first-floor House corridors, which had never been decorated. Cox used the opportunity to chart the development of the United States and the U.S. Congress, painting murals depicting all of the different buildings where Congress had met, the history of the Capitol, and the expansion of the original thirteen colonies to the Pacific. Six of his ceiling murals depict African Americans: *Iron Foundry, Circa 1850; Lincoln's Second Inaugural, 1865; Women's Suffrage Parade, 1917; Capitol Site Selection, 1791; Civil Rights Bill Passes, 1866;* and *Sharecroppers.* Three of these murals can be found in the Great Experiment Hall, so named because many of the murals chronicle the country's legislative accomplishments.

In *Iron Foundry, Circa 1850,* African Americans are featured to the right side, standing around a cotton gin. The scene is supposed to represent the change from hand labor to mechanization, but it also represents the eventual end of slavery. The cotton gin made cotton lucrative in the South by increasing the quantity of cotton that could be produced. This increased the need for African-American slaves, which ultimately led to the beginning of the Civil War and the end of slavery in the United States.

Lincoln's Second Inaugural, 1865 is the next in the series in the Great Experiment Hall. The center of the mural depicts Lincoln at his 1865 inaugural in front of the newly completed Capitol, where he said, "With malice toward none; with charity for all; with firmness in the right, as God gives us to see the right, let us strive on to finish the work we are in." To the right of Lincoln is an emancipated black man casting his vote, a result of the Civil War and the Fifteenth Amendment to the Constitution: "The right of citizens of the United States to vote shall not be denied or abridged by the United States or by any State on account of race, color, or previous condition of servitude." It is believed that more African-American men voted per capita in the years after the Fifteenth Amendment passed in 1870 than do today.

The final panel in this group is *Women's Suffrage Parade, 1917*. While African-American men (in practice) received the right to vote in 1870, women did not receive a constitutional right to vote until the Nineteenth Amendment in 1920. The African-American interest in this panel is once again to the right, next to the depiction of the New York suffrage parade in 1917. That's where we see what is probably the first depiction in the Capitol of Representative Joseph Rainey, a Republican from South Carolina, the first African American to serve in the House of Representatives. Rainey, whose portrait is on the Capitol's third floor, was the longest-serving black lawmaker until the 1950s.

Two more murals with depictions of African Americans appear in the Hall of Capitols. One of these murals is *Capitol Site Selection, 1791,* which is a portrayal of President George Washington and French designer Pierre L'Enfant discussing the plans for Washington, D.C. Washington is on his horse looking at L'Enfant, who is showing him his ideas for the new "Federal City." Standing next to L'Enfant, holding his horse, is an unidentified black man, presumably a slave. While there are no records of L'Enfant being a slave owner, Washington held as many as 316 slaves at his Mount Vernon estate in Virginia, releasing them only after the death of his wife Martha.

The next mural in the Hall of Capitols is *Civil Rights Bill Passes, 1866,* an illustration of lobbyists outside the House chambers discussing the passage of legislation thwarting Southern states' attempt to curtail African Americans' rights at the end of the Civil War. The most prominent African American in the scene is identified as Henry Highland Garnet, a well-known black abolitionist. Garnet was one of the first blacks allowed to enter the Capitol and was the first to speak before Congress. He delivered a sermon to the House of Representatives on February 12, 1865, on the end to slavery. He also was U.S. minister to Liberia, where he died in 1882.

The corridor called Westward Expansion contains the sixth representation of African Americans, *Sharecroppers*. The murals in this corridor were completed after Cox's death but were based on his preliminary sketches for the area. The

The Capitol

The Capitol currently has four floors, three of which are accessible to the public on tours and official business. Visitors can get free thirty- to forty-minute guided tours of the building through the Capitol Guide Service from Monday through Saturday, 9:00 a.m. to 4:30 p.m. (the final tour begins at 3:30 p.m.). The tours are on a first-come, first-served basis, and the building is closed to the public on Sunday and on New Year's Day, Thanksgiving Day, and Christmas Day. With the Capitol being a working legislative building, visitation guidelines can change on a daily basis because of security or political concerns. Check www.aoc.gov/cc/visit/index.cfm for up-to-date information, or call the Capitol Guide Service Recorded Information Line at 202-225-6827 before visiting.

You can tell whether the House and Senate are in session by looking for the flags flying over their respective wings. If an American flag can be seen on the Senate or House flagpole, that body is in session. If the flagpole is empty, it is not.

Your senators or representative can also schedule a tour of the Capitol for a group. These tours, which are led by members of that official's staff, are scheduled exclusively by that office and must be scheduled in advance.

All visitors to the Capitol will have to go through a security screening by the U.S. Capitol Police. Security Screening will include a magnetometer and/or security searches of all people. All items brought into the building will be screened by an X-ray device. Items that are prohibited include aerosol and nonaerosol sprays, cans and bottles, food and beverages, oversized suitcases, duffle bags and oversized backpacks, knives of any length, razors and box cutters, as well as mace and pepper spray. Firearms, incidentally, are illegal in the entire District of Columbia.

Architect of the Capitol commissioned Jeff Greene to complete this corridor, and Greene collaborated with the Architect's office and the United States Capitol Historical Society to expand on Cox's ideas with additions like *The Pony Express* and *Sharecroppers*.

Sharecropping is a form of farming where workers farm land they do not own in exchange for money or part of the crops produced. After the Civil War it became another form of slavery for some African Americans. Black sharecroppers found that no matter how hard they worked, they would always owe the sometimes unscrupulous landowner more money than they could pay, keeping them on the land for another year and giving the white landowners another year of cheap labor. This continued until mechanization allowed landowners to farm huge plots of land without human help, and many of the sharecroppers were kicked off the land and had to find other jobs.

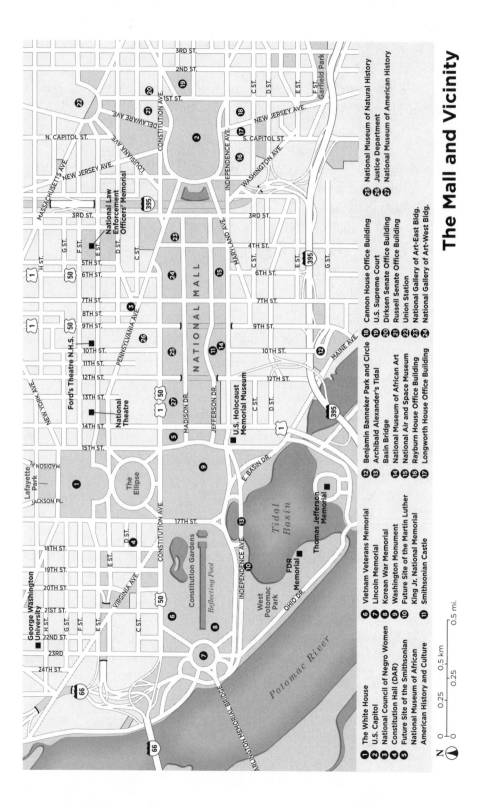

The Mall and Vicinity

1. The White House
2. U.S. Capitol
3. National Council of Negro Women
4. Constitution Hall (DAR)
5. Future Site of the Smithsonian National Museum of African American History and Culture
6. Vietnam Veterans Memorial
7. Lincoln Memorial
8. Korean War Memorial
9. Washington Monument
10. Future Site of the Martin Luther King Jr. National Memorial
11. Smithsonian Castle
12. Benjamin Banneker Park and Circle
13. Archibald Alexander's Tidal Basin Bridge
14. National Museum of African Art
15. National Air and Space Museum
16. Rayburn House Office Building
17. Longworth House Office Building
18. Cannon House Office Building
19. U.S. Supreme Court
20. Dirksen Senate Office Building
21. Russell Senate Office Building
22. Union Station
23. National Gallery of Art–East Bldg.
24. National Gallery of Art–West Bldg.
25. National Museum of Natural History
26. Justice Department
27. National Museum of American History

N

0   0.25   0.5 km

0   0.25   0.5 mi.

CHAPTER TWO

The NATIONAL MALL

What Everyone Already Knows

The National Mall can truly be called America's front yard. Stretching almost two miles and covering more than three hundred acres, the open-air avenue Mall is the center of almost every tourist's visit to Washington, D.C.

And no wonder! The Mall has it all. For nature buffs, there's sunrise at the U.S. Capitol, sunset at the Lincoln Memorial, and millions of the world-famous cherry blossoms surrounding the Tidal Basin in the spring. History lovers can find the original Declaration of Independence, Constitution, and Bill of Rights in the nearby National Archives. There are also dozens of museums and memorials honoring everything from American art and history to the nation's wars and armed conflicts to four of the nation's greatest presidents. For the politically astute, the Mall houses the headquarters of two of the three branches of the American government—the White House and the U.S. Capitol—with the Supreme Court only steps away. That rarified positioning also has made the Mall the perfect place for protests, celebrations, and rallies of all kinds, from the historic 1963 March on Washington to annual Fourth of July fireworks and parades. There's even something for sports fans: acres of wide, grassy open spaces that are good for the occasional game of softball, dodgeball, touch football, or maybe even a round of ultimate Frisbee.

The National Mall is truly our country's "Grand Avenue," where Americans go to honor our country's history and raise their voices to influence its future.

The National Mall Was the Best Place in Town to Sell Slaves

Today's National Mall is a lush green oasis of museums, monuments, and buildings running through the center of the most powerful city in the world—a place

where Americans feel welcome to celebrate and pay homage to their country's history and future. But the Mall hasn't always been so welcoming, especially to African Americans. In fact, it was the last place any black person wanted to be; before the Civil War and the Emancipation Proclamation, the National Mall claimed some of the most infamous slave markets of Washington, D.C.

While the District of Columbia had fewer slaves than Maryland or Virginia (Washington, D.C., had at the most 3,185 slaves, while there were 400,000 slaves living in Virginia and another 100,000 in Maryland before the Civil War), its unique position on the Potomac River made it perfect for the sale of human beings to the Deep South. According to one federal report, "the District of Columbia, too small for slave rearing itself, served as depot for the purchase of interstate traders, who combed Maryland and northern Virginia for slaves." The slaves would then be put on slave ships headed for places like New Orleans in the Deep South, where they could be sold for even greater profit.

Englishman Joseph Surge called Washington, D.C., "the chief seat of the American slave trade." In his book *A Visit to the United States in 1841,* he said the District of Columbia was "one of the best supplied and most frequented slave marts in the world. . . . From its locality, and from its importance as the centre of public affairs, the District of Columbia has become the focus of this dreadful traffic, which almost vies with the African slave trade itself in extent and cruelty." And the National Mall was the best place in town for slave owners to showcase their wares.

There were almost no buildings on the Mall in the 1800s—just acres and acres of grass and trees between the White House, the Capitol, and the still-under-construction Washington Monument. In fact, the District had to pass a special law in 1826 to force farmers to stop driving their cattle and livestock down to the center of the city to graze on the lush Mall grass. Slaves also could often be seen herded across the National Mall, some heading to Alexandria,

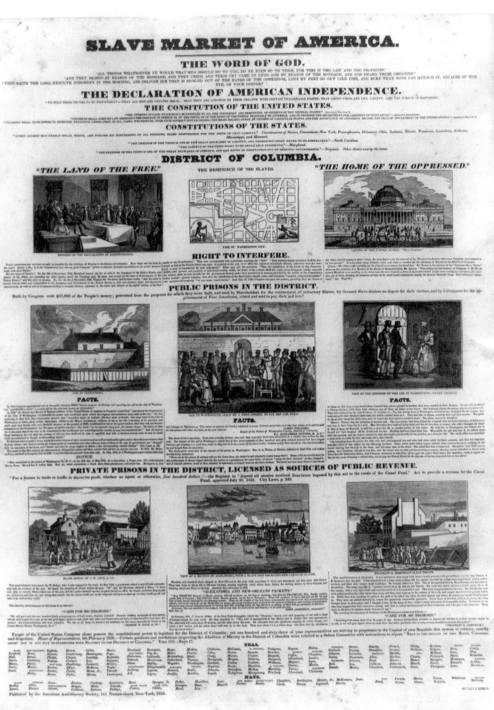

SLAVE MARKET OF AMERICA.

THE WORD OF GOD.

THE DECLARATION OF AMERICAN INDEPENDENCE.

THE CONSTITUTION OF THE UNITED STATES.

CONSTITUTIONS OF THE STATES.

DISTRICT OF COLUMBIA.

"THE LAND OF THE FREE." THE RESIDENCE OF 7000 SLAVES. "THE HOME OF THE OPPRESSED."

RIGHT TO INTERFERE.

PUBLIC PRISONS IN THE DISTRICT.

FACTS.   **FACTS.**

PRIVATE PRISONS IN THE DISTRICT, LICENSED AS SOURCES OF PUBLIC REVENUE.

Virginia, for sale and others toward the slave pens and markets that quickly sprang up around the edges of the Mall. While slave markets and pens were scattered all around the District of Columbia—including near the White House (Lafayette Tavern on F Street between Thirteenth and Fourteenth NW near the White House) and in Georgetown (McCandless Tavern near the southwest corner of Wisconsin Avenue and M Street NW)—the best known were located near or on the National Mall.

For example, the area now known as Potomac Park—the 720 riverside acres divided by the famous cherry-blossom-lined Tidal Basin—once teemed with slave pens. Another slave market and pen called Lloyd's Tavern sat at the southwest corner of Seventh and Pennsylvania Avenue NW (where the National Archives is located today). One of the occurrences it is remembered for is the sale of a young girl named Margaret, who was seized from her master and sold because her master was too far behind in his rent.

One of the more notorious slave markets in the National Mall area was known as the Yellow House, a three-story brick building painted yellow and owned by William H. Williams. Williams's marketing in slaves at the Yellow House was so profitable that he was eventually able to use the money he was making to purchase two slave ships, the *Tribune* and the *Uncas,* to transport slaves between the District and New Orleans.

What happened in most of the District's slave pens remains undocumented. However, there is a graphic description of conditions inside the Yellow House, which sat between Seventh and Eighth Streets SW right off of Independence Avenue SW (the current location of the Federal Aviation Administration building). Solomon Northup, a free black man from New York who was kidnapped and sold into slavery in Washington, D.C., experienced the Yellow House first-hand and described it in his book, *Twelve Years a Slave: Narrative of Solomon Northup, A Citizen of New-York Kidnapped in Washington City in 1841 and Rescued in 1853, from a Cotton Plantation Near the Red River in Louisiana.*

From aboveground, the Yellow House looked like any other house in the District. But belowground it was completely different. After being kidnapped, Northup got his first look at the Yellow House when two men came in to tell him his new lot in life as a slave. Inside, the slaves were forced to stay in dank, musty underground rooms with small windows secured with iron bars, or they were placed in rooms with no windows at all. The only furnishings were an old, dirty stove, a wooden bench, and rings on the wall and in the floor to which slaves' arms and legs could be chained.

Outside was a thirty-square-foot yard enclosed by a twelve-foot brick wall, complete with a heavy iron door separating it from the street. A roof was attached to one side of the wall. The Yellow House was "like a farmer's barnyard in most respects, save it was so constructed that the outside world could never see the human cattle that were herded there," Northup wrote. The brick wall hid most of what went on inside. "A stranger looking at it, would never have dreamed of its execrable uses," Northup concluded. "Strange as it may seem, within plain sight of this same house, looking down from its commanding height upon it, was the Capitol. The voices of patriotic representatives boasting of freedom and equality, and the rattling of the poor slave's chains, almost commingled. A slave pen within the very shadow of the Capitol!"

The Yellow House wasn't even the closest slave pen to the Capitol. The Saint Charles Hotel, sitting three blocks from the Capitol at the corner of Third Street and Pennsylvania Avenue NW, advertised its elaborate basement "slave pens" to its clientele of rich southern slave owners. While they wined and dined upstairs, the hotel promised that their slaves would be "well cared for." The hotel even offered a money-back guarantee if a slave escaped one of its six thirty-foot-long arched cells with iron doors and iron wall rings and chains. The hotel's notice read: IN CASE OF ESCAPE, FULL VALUE OF THE NEGRO WILL BE PAID BY THE PROPRIETOR.

Edward S. Abdy, visiting the young United States, described yet another National Mall slave pen and market in his book *Journal of a Residence and Tour in the United States of North America, from April, 1833, to October, 1834.*

> It is surrounded by a wooden paling fourteen or fifteen feet in height, with the posts outside to prevent escape and separated from the building by a space too narrow to admit of a free circulation of air. At a small window above, which was unglazed and exposed alike to the heat of summer and the cold of winter, so trying to the constitution, two or three sable faces appeared, looking out wistfully to while away the time and catch a refreshing breeze; the weather being extremely hot. In this wretched hovel, all colors, except white—the only guilty one—both sexes, and all ages, are confined, exposed indiscriminately to all the contamination which may be expected in such society and under such seclusion.

A public garden near the Department of Education that may have been the site of Robey's Tavern.

Abdy was describing Robey's Slave Pen and Tavern, one of the most notorious National Mall slave pens. It was located in a spot that is currently occupied by a garden in between the Department of Education and the Federal Aviation Administration buildings on the east side of Seventh Street between Maryland and Independence Avenue SW. Ironically, this is only a block away from today's Smithsonian Institution National Museum of African Art.

Business was booming at Robey's. A newspaper article in *The Washington Spectator* on December 4, 1830, described seeing "a drove consisting of males and females chained in couples, starting from Robey's tavern on foot, for Alexandria, where with others, they are to embark on board a slave-ship in waiting to convey them to the South."

There are other firsthand accounts of what went on at Robey's, such as this abolitionist report:

In May, 1834, a gentleman visited it, and fell into conversation with the overseer of the pen. He heard the clanking of chains within the pen. "O," said the overseer—himself a slave, "I have seen fifty or seventy slaves taken out of the pen, and the males chained together in pairs, and drove off to the south—and how they would cry, and groan, and take on, and wring their hands, but the driver would put on the whip, and tell them to shut up—so that they would go off, and bear it as well as they could."

Cruelty was the norm at Robey's. Abdy wrote, "While I was in the city, Robey had got possession of a woman, whose term of slavery was limited to six years. It was expected that she would be sold before the expiration of that period, and sent away to a distance, where the assertion of her claim would subject her to ill-usage. Cases of this kind are very common."

A second scene from Abdy's book tells us more about the tavern itself and the dangers that even free blacks faced. A free black woman had left her papers identifying herself as such with a man named Judge Hooper of Centerville, Maryland. Her employer talked her into leaving her husband and family to get her papers back so that she could not be kidnapped and sold into slavery. However, it turned out that this was a plot devised by her employer and his friend so that *they* could kidnap her. The kidnappers then brought her to the District of Columbia and Robey's Tavern. Abdy reported:

> Here she was purchased by a notorious fellow of the name of Simson, and imprisoned in a room destined to such purposes in Robey's tavern; where she was brutally flogged, because she would not give up the name of a friend, (a white,) who had been to see her. The person from whom I had this account, the wife of one of those benevolent men alluded to as the friends of the oppressed, obtained an interview with her; and a letter having been dispatched to Centreville in Virginia, an answer was received that no such person was known there. It was too late when this mistake was rectified.

The woman was shipped to New Orleans, where Simson likely sold her into slavery.

Today, there's no trace of slave markets or pens on the Mall. The Saint Charles Hotel was torn down in 1924. The Yellow House and Robey's Tavern were closed down after the Civil War, with nothing left behind to prove that thousands of slaves suffered terribly while inside these buildings. Perhaps someday the District will put up a marker commemorating those whose lives were forever changed on the National Mall.

The Lincoln Memorial

The Lincoln Memorial was the second major Washington monument erected to honor President Abraham Lincoln after his assassination (the statue in Lincoln Park in Capitol Hill was the first). Dedicated in 1922, the memorial features a depiction of an African American in a mural above the Gettysburg Address. *Emancipation* was one of two murals painted by Jules Guerin that primarily serve as a backdrop for the massive statue of Abraham Lincoln that sits in the middle of the memorial. *Emancipation* shows an angel representing Truth freeing a slave. The angel and slave are flanked by groups of figures representing Justice and Immortality.

Marian Anderson's Free Concert. Two of the most important events in African-American history happened on the steps of the Lincoln Memorial. The first took place over Easter weekend in 1939, when African-American singer Marian Anderson climbed the steps of the Lincoln Memorial to give a free concert. Each note Anderson sang was an act of defiance against racism.

The world-famous singer known for her velvety contralto voice had performed for royalty in Europe and for presidents in the United States, but the Daughters of the American Revolution had refused to let her perform at Constitution Hall because of her skin color. Anderson had been contracted by Howard University to perform a benefit concert at its school of music on Easter Sunday weekend. But once word got out that the amazingly gifted Marian Anderson was performing at Howard, the throngs of people expected to try to attend would have overwhelmed the seating that was available at the private African-American university.

To accommodate the expected crowd, Howard officials asked the Daughters of the American Revolution to allow them to use the 4,000-seat Constitution Hall, home of the National Symphony and one of the top musical venues in the country. However, every date that the Howard officials asked for was already booked. Suspecting that something was amiss, Anderson's manager asked a white performer to call Constitution Hall and attempt to book the same dates that the Howard officials had tried to book for Anderson. When the white performer called, the same dates that Constitution Hall officials said were closed were magically open again. When confronted about their duplicity, the Daughters of the American Revolution finally came out and said that they would not allow Marian

Lincoln Memorial

Anderson to perform at Constitution Hall because their organization did not rent the hall to African-American artists.

One of Anderson's friends, First Lady Eleanor Roosevelt, decided that it was time to take a public stand against racism. (Anderson, by this time, had performed once at the White House for the president and first lady, who loved her voice so much that they invited her back to perform for the visiting king and queen of England.) Once Eleanor Roosevelt heard that the Daughters of the American Revolution refused to let Anderson perform in Constitution Hall, she immediately resigned her membership to the group. In a newspaper column, Mrs. Roosevelt said that to remain a member of a group that had decided to ban black artists from their venue "implies approval of that action."

In addition to embarrassing the group by publicly resigning, Mrs. Roosevelt took it upon herself to find another venue in which Anderson could perform. At the suggestion of the NAACP's executive secretary Walter White, Mrs. Roosevelt obtained approval for Anderson to perform at the Lincoln Memorial and rallied government officials to attend the Easter Sunday concert.

Marian Anderson

By the time the concert began that evening, more than seventy-five thousand people, black and white, had gathered at the foot of the Lincoln Memorial steps, and hundreds of thousands of others sat intently by their radios to wait for Marian Anderson's first song. Taking a deep breath, Anderson had the crowd enraptured from her first lines of "My Country 'Tis of Thee" to the end of her final song, "Nobody Knows the Trouble I've Seen." Once she finished, thunderous applause rang out on the National Mall, and so many people wanted to shake her hand that Anderson had to be escorted from the Lincoln Memorial.

Anderson's concert at the Lincoln Memorial had a profound effect on the country, including, eventually, the people who had refused to let her perform at Constitution Hall. Four years after her Lincoln Memorial performance, the Daughters of the American Revolution formally apologized to Anderson and invited her to perform at Constitution Hall in front of an integrated audience.

The Anderson concert gave birth to a tradition of using the Lincoln Memorial as a place to fight racism and endorse peace and civil rights, and in 1963 an integrated crowd at the memorial heard one of the greatest speeches in American history from a young civil rights activist named Martin Luther King Jr.

"I Have a Dream." Martin Luther King Jr.'s 1963 "I Have a Dream" speech during the March on Washington for Jobs and Freedom is universally recognized as one of the most powerful, influential, and historically important speeches ever given in the United States. In what was then the largest protest in D.C. history, more than 250,000 people, both black and white, showed up to call for civil rights around the nation. Artists such as Marian Anderson performed for the crowd from their perch at the Lincoln Memorial, while leaders such as Georgia congressman John Lewis, who was then a leader of the Student Nonviolent Coordinating Committee, called for equality now. King's speech, however, was the highlight of the day.

Starting with prepared remarks, King called for Americans to allow everyone to fulfill their country's promise of "life, liberty and the pursuit of happiness," but then he moved to a theme he had broached before—"I Have a Dream": "I have a dream that one day this nation will rise up and live out the true meaning of its creed: 'We hold these truths to be self-evident: that all men are created equal,'" King said, electrifying the crowd. "I have a dream that my four children will one day live in a nation where they will not be judged by the color of their skin but by the content of their character."

King wrapped up by speaking directly about the promise of America:

> When we allow freedom to ring, when we let it ring from every village and every hamlet, from every state and every city, we will be able to speed up that day when all of God's children, black men and white men, Jews and Gentiles, Protestants and Catholics, will be able to join hands and sing in the words of the old Negro spiritual: Free at last, free at last. Thank God almighty, we are free at last.

King's speech cemented his reputation around the world, leading him to be named *Time* magazine's Man of the Year for 1963 and making him the youngest person to be awarded the Nobel Peace Prize, which he received in 1964.

To honor King and his speech, in 2003 the National Park Service placed an inscribed marble pedestal at the Lincoln Memorial to commemorate the location of the speech. The pedestal, which sits on the exact spot where Dr. King stood to deliver the "I Have a Dream" speech is inscribed: I HAVE A DREAM; MARTIN LUTHER KING, JR.; THE MARCH ON WASHINGTON FOR JOBS AND FREEDOM; AUGUST 23, 1963.

The inscription can be found centered in the middle of the granite steps, eighteen steps down from the chamber. The inscription is oriented so that visitors reading it will face the same direction that King did when he gave the speech and so that they will look out upon the same vista he did: the Reflecting Pool, the Washington Monument, the Capitol, and the Mall.

The Korean War Veterans Memorial

The Korean War Veterans Memorial honors those who fought in the very first conflict in which all of America's sons and daughters battled together as a united whole instead of being racially segregated. The memorial itself shows this integration, featuring statues of twelve white soldiers, three African Americans, two Hispanics, an Asian, and a Native American. The soldiers represent one unit, composed of all of the armed services that fought in Korea. The African-American statues depict an Army BAR gunner, an Army rifleman carrying an M-1 Garand Rifle, and a Marine medical corpsman. They are located in positions 4, 6, and 14 from the front. While there are only nineteen soldiers in the unit, their reflections can be seen in the black granite Mural Wall, making a total of thirty-eight soldiers representing the 38th Parallel and the thirty-eight months of the war.

African-American veterans from the Korean War have also been honored by a plaque at Arlington National Cemetery.

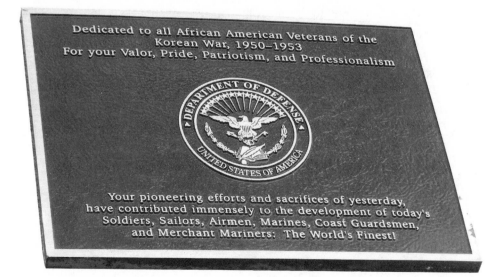

Dedicated to all African American Veterans of the Korean War, 1950–1953
For your Valor, Pride, Patriotism, and Professionalism

DEPARTMENT OF DEFENSE
UNITED STATES OF AMERICA

Your pioneering efforts and sacrifices of yesterday, have contributed immensely to the development of today's Soldiers, Sailors, Airmen, Marines, Coast Guardsmen, and Merchant Mariners: The World's Finest!

Desegregation of the Armed Forces

In 1948 President Harry S. Truman ended formal racial segregation in the armed forces with an executive order. African-American soldiers who had been forced to serve in subservient positions or segregated units in earlier conflicts slowly flooded into Korea as regular members of the U.S. armed forces. In Korea 3,075 African Americans gave their lives.

MORE FACTS

Many African Americans can also be found in the Mural Wall, which features more than 2,400 images of the Army, Navy, Marine Corps, Air Force, and Coast Guard personnel and their equipment. When viewed from a distance, the pictures on the Mural Wall blend into an outline of the mountain range in Korea that the soldiers had to overcome. Capping it all is the Pool of Remembrance and its inscription: OUR NATION HONORS HER SONS AND DAUGHTERS WHO ANSWERED THE CALL TO DEFEND A COUNTRY THEY NEVER KNEW AND A PEOPLE THEY NEVER MET.

Since some were unwilling to accept mandated desegregation, some units still consisted solely of black men. As a result, the first American victory of the Korean conflict belonged to African-American troops. The all-black troops of L Company, 24th Infantry Regiment, 25th Infantry Division, U.S. Eighth Army, recaptured the town of Yechon, killing at least 258 North Koreans. Two Americans were killed and a handful were wounded in action. Newspapers across America blared the fact that the first victory of the Korean conflict had been won by "Negroes," while other U.S. and U.N. troops had been forced to retreat.

African-American soldiers went on to gain other honors during the Korean conflict, including Army Pvt. William H. Thompson, who won the Congressional Medal of Honor in 1950. Thompson single-handedly manned a machine-gun nest to allow his troop mates to retreat to safety. The effort cost Thompson his life. Navy Ensign Jesse L. Brown, the very first African-American naval aviator, won the Distinguished Flying Cross. Brown was awarded this medal for dangerous combat actions he took that cost him his life. Brown had been providing close-air support for units of the 7th Marines during the Chosin Reservoir breakout in December 1950. In 1972 the Navy named one of its escort ships the USS *Jesse Brown*.

The Vietnam Veterans Memorial, the Three Soldiers Statue, and the Vietnam Women's Memorial

The Vietnam Veterans Memorial serves as a reminder and a tribute to those who fought and died overseas in the Vietnam War, the most divisive conflict for Americans since the Civil War. It was only fitting, then, that the memorial designed to honor those who fought in Vietnam was controversial as well.

The names of the 58,249 American men and women who died or are missing as a result of the Vietnam conflict are carved into a black granite wall. (Eight women, seven Army nurses, and one Air Force nurse are memorialized on the wall. The rest are men.) Today the Vietnam Veterans Memorial is considered striking and emotional. Millions of people have visited it to view a loved one's name, to make rubbings to take home, to leave offerings, or just to touch the black granite and whisper a prayer.

But when the design was first approved, many Vietnam veterans and supporters hated the idea of a simple black wall with carved names serving as their memorial. They wanted something like other war memorials, with statues and flags and plaques extolling the virtue of those who fought. Their protests became so vocal that then–interior secretary James Watt initially refused to allow the construction of the Vietnam Veterans Memorial on the National Mall.

A compromise was finally reached when the design was revised to include a flagpole and a bronze statue called the *Three Soldiers* or the *Three Servicemen*. Erected in 1984, two years after the Vietnam Veterans Memorial opened, the larger-than-life group of statues stands in a grove of trees near the west entrance to the wall. The statues show three young men wearing Vietnam War–era military uniforms and carrying infantry weapons. They are depicted walking as if clearing a jungle canopy. Sculptor Frederick Hart described the statues on his Web site: "I see the wall as a kind of ocean, a sea of sacrifice that is overwhelming and nearly incomprehensible in the sweep of names. I place these figures upon the shore of that sea, gazing upon it, standing vigil before it, reflecting the human face of it, the human heart."

Vietnam Veterans Memorial

The statues depict a lead soldier, modeled after a white twenty-one-year-old Marine, flanked by a Cuban-American soldier carrying a machine gun on his shoulder. The final figure in the statue group is that of a young African-American soldier, a composite of several different African-American men used as models.

It was appropriate that Hart included an African-American soldier in the group. While the Korean conflict marked the first time black soldiers served in nonsegregated units, the Vietnam conflict marked the first time the number of African-American soldiers in a conflict reached parity with the American population. The Pentagon estimated that approximately 12 percent of the combat deaths in Vietnam, or more than seven thousand, were among blacks, almost exactly the percentage of blacks in the American population. And those African Americans served honorably, with twenty men winning Medals of Honor.

The first African American to sacrifice his life in the Vietnam War was

Army Pvt. 1st Class Milton Lee Olive III of the 3rd Platoon, Company B, 2nd Battalion, 503rd Infantry, 173rd Airborne Brigade. The first combat-ready major platoon to arrive in Vietnam, the paratroopers known as the "Sky Soldiers" landed in Vietnam in 1963. Two years later, Olive and his troop mates were pursuing Viet Cong through the jungle when one threw a hand grenade in the midst of Olive and four other American soldiers. Olive saw the grenade and fell on it, absorbing the blast with his body. The Mississippi native's selfless action saved the other four members of this group, and President Lyndon Johnson presented his family with a posthumous Medal of Honor at the White House six months later.

African-American women also served honorably in Vietnam, although they served in smaller numbers. The black women who served in the Vietnam conflict are not specifically represented among the three figures that make up the Vietnam Women's Memorial. It was added to the Vietnam Veteran Memorial site in 1993, making it the very first memorial in the nation's capital honoring women's military service.

Approximately 265,500 American women served around the world during the Vietnam conflict. The majority of women who served in Vietnam were nurses, a profession African-American women had been engaged in for the American military for years. (African-American nurses served unofficially in the military during the Civil War, the Spanish American War, World War I, and World War II.)

One of the African-American women who showed exceptional bravery during the Vietnam conflict was Lt. Diane M. Lindsay, who became the first black woman to be awarded the Soldier's Medal for heroism. While working in the 95th Evacuation Hospital in Da Nang, a confused soldier attempted to set off a grenade at the hospital compound. He pulled the pin, but Lt. Lindsay rushed over and, with the help of a male soldier, convinced the berserk soldier to surrender the grenade. Because of her quick thinking and heroic action, she was awarded the Soldier's Medal for heroism and promoted to captain.

Archibald Alexander's Tidal Basin Bridge

The Tidal Basin is one of America's favorite places to be in the springtime. More than seven hundred thousand people come to Washington each year to see the world-famous Japanese pink and white cherry trees in bloom on the shores of

Tidal Basin bridge designed and built by Archibald Alexander with Washington Memorial in the background

the basin. The cherry trees made their first appearance in Washington in 1912 as a gift to the capital city from the people of Japan. The wife of President William Howard Taft and Viscountess Chinda of Japan together planted the first trees on the banks of the Tidal Basin.

More than 3,700 cherry trees bloom in the Tidal Basin area each spring. Visitors find some of the best views of the blossoms from the Tidal Basin Bridge (a three-lane structure that allows vehicles and pedestrians to use Independence Avenue to cross the north side of the Tidal Basin) and the Tidal Basin seawall (which holds the Potomac Rivers waters back from the National Mall and provides two miles' worth of walking distance around the basin). These views would

not exist without the efforts of an African-American engineer named Archibald Alphonso Alexander (1888–1958).

Born in Ottuma, Iowa, Archibald "Archie" Alexander was the first African American to earn an engineering degree from the University of Iowa. He was awarded the degree in 1912. Alexander also helped integrate the school's football team, earning the nickname "Alexander the Great" because of his skills on the gridiron. An interesting side note to Alexander's career: Alexander was the only black player on the University of Iowa's football team. In 1910, neighboring University of Missouri said it would refuse to play Iowa if Alexander was allowed to play. Fearing a riot, the Iowa coaches left Alexander behind when they traveled to Missouri to play. Without their star tackle, Iowa lost 5-0 (a 3-point field goal and a 2-point safety). Because of the loss and the insult to one of his players, Iowa coach Jesse Hawley swore never to field another team against Missouri. The university has kept Hawley's promise, and the two universities have not played football against each other since.

This would not be Alexander's only brush with racism. Despite his intellectual and athletic skills, Alexander was bluntly told by one of his white professors that a Negro would never be able to find a job as an engineer. Alexander ignored that warning and worked his way up from an entry-level position at the Marsh Engineering Firm. Within two years, Alexander's skills made him the natural choice to be placed in charge of many of the firm's projects.

Alexander decided to strike out on his own in 1914, opening A. A. Alexander Inc. in Des Moines, Iowa. Three years later, Alexander and a white classmate, George F. Higbee, decided to work together and form an engineering company specializing in building bridges, viaducts, and sewage systems throughout Iowa. Alexander continued to lead the company after Higbee died in a 1925 construction accident.

In 1929 another Iowa classmate, Maurice Repass, joined Alexander as a junior partner, and they renamed the firm Alexander and Repass. They were so successful that in 1949 *Ebony* magazine named them the nation's "most successful interracial business." Alexander and Repass were awarded the contract for building the $11 million Tidal Basin Bridge and seawall in pre–World War II Washington. According to local newspaper reports, Alexander personally took control of the project and hired both blacks and whites to work on the bridge and seawall. The *Washington Eagle* newspaper noted in May 1943 that "Alexander, the senior partner, is supervising the Tidal Basin job which now employs 160 Negro and white mechanics and laborers."

Completed on time and on budget, Alexander's work would springboard Alexander and Repass to other work in the District, including the construction of the elevated Whitehurst Freeway, which runs over the upscale Georgetown harbor district. Alexander would work with the Alexander and Repass firm until his death, but his talents also ran in other directions. He lectured extensively at Howard University in Washington, D.C., and also served on its board; won the NAACP's highest award, the Spingarn Award; served as national president of Kappa Alpha Psi fraternity; and was appointed by President Dwight Eisenhower as the first Republican governor of the Virgin Islands.

When visiting the Tidal Basin or looking at images of the cherry blossoms in bloom, look for Alexander's bridge in the background, an enduring symbol of one man's perseverance and intelligence.

Benjamin Banneker Park and Banneker Circle

Benjamin Banneker Overlook Park and Banneker Circle provide a tranquil transition from the hustle and bustle of the National Mall to the more serene Southwest Waterfront. The park, the first public space in Washington, D.C., to be named after an African American, features a commemorative fountain, a view of the waterfront, and a panoramic outlook of the National Mall and its monuments.

The park is named after Benjamin Banneker, the nation's first recognized African-American scientist, who helped determine the boundaries of the District of Columbia in 1791. Banneker Circle is one of the few circles in Washington, D.C., without a statue, but the steward of the circle, the Washington Interdependence Council, is working on placing a statue of Banneker in the park to commemorate his contributions to the nation.

Benjamin Banneker

Benjamin Banneker is known as one of America's first and foremost inventors, astronomers, scientists, engineers, and publishers. In an early example of his skill and intellect, a twenty-two-year-old Banneker designed a wooden clock in 1753 that struck every hour on the hour for fifty years. He was also the first African American and one of the first Americans to publish an almanac, and he was one of the first astronomers to document that the star Sirius was in fact a double star.

MORE FACTS

Banneker Park and Banneker Circle lie in an area that has figured prominently in the history of African Americans: During the late 1770s, the overlook was originally part of a plantation belonging to Notely Young, whose house was on the site and who reportedly owned 265 slaves. The park also overlooks the Southwest Washington Waterfront, which was the site of the near escape in 1848 of seventy-seven slaves aboard the coastal schooner *Pearl*.

In June 1970 the District of Columbia's Redevelopment Land Agency transferred 4.68 acres of the Banneker Overlook site to the U.S. government, and on November 19, 1971, a park was created on the site and designated as the Benjamin Banneker Overlook Park. Daniel Urban Kiley, one of America's most recognized landscape architects who was also responsible for the grounds at the United States Air Force Academy and the Dalle Centrale at La Defense in Paris, France, designed the park, which combines many granite elements, including a large fountain, trees, and lighting as a transition to the open space of the Southwest Waterfront.

African-American History in the Smithsonian Institution Museums

African Americans are an integral part of American history and life, so it is only fitting that almost all of the Smithsonian Institution museums have permanent exhibits featuring facets of African-American life.

African Americans have been part of the Smithsonian Institution since

President James K. Polk created it by signing legislation on August 10, 1846. A mere six years later, in 1852, the Smithsonian Institution hired its first African-American employee, Solomon G. Brown, who remained an institution employee for more than fifty years.

Before going to work for the Smithsonian, Brown was a key participant in one of the greatest technological breakthroughs of the nineteenth century. Brown had secured employment with the postmaster in Washington, D.C., but at that time, the post office did more than just deliver mail. It also was in charge of an experiment by esteemed scientists Joseph Henry and Samuel Morse, who were trying to prove that a telegraph could accurately and quickly send messages across the country. To prove that their telegraph would work, they needed someone to construct the poles and lay the wires between Washington and Baltimore. Brown was assigned to help, making him the only African American to witness the birth of the telegraph age. According to the 1887 book *Men of Mark: Eminent, Progressive and Rising* by the Rev. William J. Simmons, "Mr. Brown was a natural scientist, and coming in contact with these learned men only increased his thirst for knowledge." Simmons describes Brown as follows: "He is a man of rare scientific acquirements, very unassuming in his appearance, and yet his intelligence would astonish one on making his acquaintance."

Because of Henry and Morse's success, Henry was named the first secretary of the Smithsonian Institution, and he soon brought Solomon Brown along with him. Brown, who is listed in the institution's annual reports as "Clerk, In charge of Transportation," in reality held several positions at the Smithsonian, starting as a general laborer but ending up as a scientific illustrator, a naturalist, and a lecturer before the city's scientific societies.

With word of his intelligence and accomplishments spreading, Brown was often asked to speak on topics, not only to black audiences but sometimes white as well. Brown's first lecture was on January 10, 1855, before a mixed audience at a church near the Capitol building. "This lecture was called out by the request of several prominent citizens of Washington," according to Simmons, and "he was greeted by a large, intelligent audience, among whom were several white citizens." His topic was the insects of the United States, and Simmons described it as a success "as may be judged from the many times this lecture has been repeated—each time by request."

The National Museum of Natural History

Solomon Brown was present at the 1904 groundbreaking ceremony of the Smithsonian's National Museum of Natural History (the first national museum), and he finally retired from the Smithsonian in 1906. In 1994, the Smithsonian Institution planted a Cedar of Lebanon tree in his memory at the site of the National Museum of Natural History. The tree stands there to this day.

Inside the National Museum of Natural History, which today is the most visited natural history museum in the world, is the African Voices Hall, where visitors can explore the people, culture, and history of the cradle of humanity. Using more than four hundred objects from the museum's collection, the exhibition also takes advantage of photographs and video, as well as sound stations where historical and living persons tell the story of Africa and what the rest of the world can learn from its experiences.

The Hirshhorn

At the Hirshhorn Museum and Sculpture Garden, look for African-American sculptor Richard Hunt's birdlike abstraction outside in the sculpture garden.

The Woolworth's Counter

The National Museum of American History is closed for renovation until summer 2008, but some of its most important pieces have been moved to the Air and Space Museum. One of the exhibitions that has moved is that of the famous Greensboro, North Carolina, Woolworth's lunch counter. The sit-in at Woolworth's instigated by four black North Carolina Agricultural and Technical College students inspired the integration of many restaurants and stores before the passage of the Civil Rights Act of 1964. The four students caused this change by sitting down at a whites-only lunch counter and refusing to leave once they were refused service. When the Woolworth's closed without serving them, they returned the next morning with twenty-five more students. Within a year, similar demonstrations had spread to hundreds of cities in the North and South, and a new era of civil rights protesting was born.

Inside, the Smithsonian's museum of international modern and contemporary art boasts approximately 11,500 paintings, sculptures, mixed-media installations, and works on paper in its collection. Artists whose works are featured here include Sam Gilliam, Jacob Lawrence, Thornton Dial Jr., Horace Pippin, Alison Saar, and Betye Saar.

The Smithsonian National Air and Space Museum

The Smithsonian National Air and Space Museum features African Americans in the Pioneers of Flight Gallery exhibit "Black Wings: The American Black in Aviation." The exhibit features more than one hundred historical documents and memorabilia from pioneers of African-American flight (like the Tuskegee Airmen and Bessie Coleman, the first African-American pilot), as well as from the current generation of African-American flyers (like Daniel "Chappie" James Jr., the first African-American four-star general; Dr. Guion Bluford Jr., the first African-American to go into space; Mae Jemison, the first African-American woman astronaut; and Patrice Clarke-Washington, the first African-American female captain to fly for a major airline).

The Smithsonian Institution National Museum of African Art

The country's only national museum of African art, the Smithsonian Institution National Museum of African Art occupies a special place in American history. Founded in 1964 by Warren M. Robbins, who had spent a decade in Europe as a cultural attaché in the U.S. Foreign Service, the National Museum of African Art is one of the few underground museums in the United States.

Located in the Quadrangle Complex (which also houses the Arthur M. Sackler Gallery and the S. Dillon Ripley International Center) behind the Smithsonian Institution Building, 96 percent of the National Museum of African Art resides underground with the Enid A. Haupt Victorian Garden on its roof. (The garden covers 4.2 acres and is one of the largest rooftop gardens in the world.)

In addition to being one of the only underground museums, the National Museum of African Art has a distinguished history. Originally known as the Museum of African Art, it first opened in a Capitol Hill townhouse once owned by renowned abolitionist Frederick Douglass. Featuring examples of Douglass

Smithsonian Institution National Museum of African Art

memorabilia, nineteenth-century paintings by black artists, and a smattering of loaned African art, the museum eventually grew to the point where it occupied nine row houses with twelve galleries, a small auditorium, and a library. By the time the Museum of African Art became a bureau of the Smithsonian Institution in 1979, its collections included some eight thousand objects of African sculpture, costumes, textiles, musical instruments, and jewelry; numerous books on African culture and history; early maps of Africa; educational materials; and photographs, slides, and film segments on African art, society, and environment bequeathed to the museum by world-renowned photographer Eliot Elisofon.

The museum was renamed the National Museum of African Art in 1981 and moved to its current location at 950 Independence Avenue SW in 1987. The museum complex, designed by architect Jean Paul Carlhian of the Boston firm Shepley, Bulfinch, Richardson and Abbott, opened to the public on September 28, 1987.

The museum now holds more than 8,500 African art objects, including the Walt Disney-Tishman collection of textiles, photography, sculpture, pottery, paintings, and jewelry from nearly every area of the continent of Africa. It is the nation's largest publicly held collection of contemporary African art and it is continually growing, receiving an average of sixty-seven gifts per year.

In addition, the museum is the home of the Warren M. Robbins Library, which houses more than twenty thousand volumes and periodicals on African art, history, culture, and related topics, and the Eliot Elisofon Photographic Archives, which has 300,000 photographic prints and transparencies and 120,000 feet of unedited film footage on Africa.

The National Gallery of Art

Students of African-American military history and fans of the Oscar-award-winning movie *Glory*—the story of the 54th Massachusetts Volunteer Infantry Regiment, one of the first African-American Civil War regiments—must visit the National Gallery of Art.

One of the artifacts on exhibit at the gallery is the plaster cast of the Shaw Memorial, one of the greatest examples of American sculpture of the nineteenth century. The actual memorial—a work in bronze by sculptor Augustus Saint-Gaudens, who also did the Adams Memorial in the city's Rock Creek Cemetery—resides in Boston, the training ground of the 54th Massachusetts regiment. But the plaster cast housed in the National Gallery of Art's West Building is an impressive piece of artwork in itself. The bas-relief cast—fifteen feet high, eighteen feet wide, and three feet deep—is so massive that the gallery had to remove 20 feet of wall and place a massive steel beam in the floor to accommodate it.

The cast on display is not the original plaster cast; it is a second one created by Saint-Gaudens for the Paris Salon of 1898 and the Paris Exposition Universalle of 1900. It was then sent back to America for the Pan-American Exposition of 1901 in Buffalo, and it was acquired by Buffalo's Albright-Knox Art Gallery. In 1949 the plaster monument was sent to the Saint-Gaudens National Historic Site in Cornish, New Hampshire, where it was displayed in an outdoor pavilion. In 1997 it was brought to the National Gallery of Art, where it is being held on a long-time loan.

The gallery's Shaw Memorial includes profiles of Col. Robert Gould Shaw on horseback surrounded by his battle-ready soldiers and being led by drummer boys. Overhead an angel carries an olive branch and poppies, symbolizing life and death.

The real 54th Massachusetts regiment included such people as Lewis and Charles Douglass, the sons of Frederick Douglass; James Caldwell, the grandson of Sojourner Truth; and William H. Carney, the first African American to win the Medal of Honor. Despite being shot five times, Carney, from Norfolk, Virginia, did not let the U.S. flag hit the ground during the 54th Massachusetts's unsuccessful attempt to storm Fort Wagner in July 1863. A white soldier, seeing Carney's injuries, offered to hold the flag of the 54th for him, but he replied, "No one but a member of the 54th should carry the colors." Carney made it to safety, and before falling from his injuries, he told his troop mates, "Boys, I only did my duty. The flag never touched the ground."

Carney received the Medal of Honor because of his heroism, but it was not officially awarded to him until 1900, more than three decades after the battle. The American flag saved by Carney is preserved inside the Memorial Hall in Boston, and Carney can be found depicted as one of the soldiers following Colonel Shaw in the Shaw Memorial.

The National Council for Negro Women

The only African-American organization to maintain an office in the world-famous Pennsylvania Avenue corridor between the White House and the U.S. Capitol is the National Council of Negro Women (NCNW) at 633 Pennsylvania Avenue NW. Founded by Mary McLeod Bethune in 1935, the NCNW originally was located at 1318 Vermont Avenue NW in what is now the Bethune Council House, which today houses the Bethune Museum and Archives, the only archives devoted to black women's history in the United States. Using the equity from the Bethune Council House, the NCNW bought its current national headquarters in December 1995.

The NCNW serves as a United Nations–type organization for groups made up of African-American women. Back in 1935 McLeod Bethune said that what black women needed was not another organization, but one entity to bring all of the existing organizations together so they could work more efficiently. Thus, the NCNW was founded as an "organization of organizations." Today the National Council of Negro Women reaches nearly four million women through thirty-nine national affiliate organizations and more than 240 sections.

The Annual Black Family Reunion Celebration on the National Mall.
The National Council for Negro Women's signature event is the Black Family
Reunion Celebration, held annually on the National Mall in the fall. The two-
day celebration is recognized as the largest and most significant family event in
the nation and regularly attracts more than five hundred thousand participants
to its booths, concerts, and exhibitions set around the Washington Monument.

African Americans and others come to this free festival to celebrate the history and traditions of the black family. The festival was started in 1986 by Dr.
Dorothy I. Height, the NCNW's chair and president emerita, as a way of
strengthening the African-American family and combating negative stereotypes.
It features live music, health screenings, African-American crafts, home-buyer
workshops, and other ways to improve family life.

WHITE HOUSE

What Everyone Already Knows

The White House is the home and headquarters of the president of the United States, and it is the District of Columbia's oldest public building. It has been known by several names, including the "Presidential Palace," the "President's House," and the "Executive Mansion." The first president, George Washington, along with District of Columbia city planner Pierre L'Enfant, selected the White House site, now known as 1600 Pennsylvania Avenue NW. As with the Capitol, city planners held a competition for the design of the President's House. Irish-born architect James Hoban's design beat eight others, and construction began in 1792. The name "White House" was not be officially used until President Theodore Roosevelt coined the term in 1901. While years of renovations and improvement have changed the White House, the exterior stone walls are part of the original construction of the White House, dating back two centuries.

The First White House Chef Ran Away

George Washington is the only president who never slept in the White House,

but that doesn't mean that he didn't stay in an executive mansion. The federal government moved from New York City to Philadelphia in 1790 to await the completion of suitable federal buildings in the District of Columbia. After shuttling through several houses in New York City, President George Washington, his family, and his entourage were offered the finest mansion in Philadelphia to serve as Washington's headquarters. The three-story

Unnamed black cook in the White House kitchen   LC-USZ62-105300

house owned by Robert Morris would become the first executive mansion known as the President's House, the precursor to the District's White House.

George Washington and his successor John Adams both lived in and operated the early days of the presidency from Robert Morris's mansion in Philadelphia, which also brought about the first African-American connections to the presidency. As a slave owner, Washington brought eight slaves with him from his home at Mount Vernon to Philadelphia. These slaves, Oney Judge, Moll, Austin, Hercules, Richmond, Giles, Paris, Christopher Sheels, and Joe (a ninth slave who joined them later), were the first blacks to work for the presidency and live in the executive mansion. Some of these slaves became famous in their own right.

Hercules, the President's Chef. Hercules, for example, became known as the first presidential chef. In addition to being known as one of the finest chefs in the thirteen colonies, he also supervised the kitchen for all of the entertaining the president did at Mount Vernon and at the President's House in Philadelphia. Hercules was so well respected that Washington allowed him to run his own business out of the kitchen, which allowed the slave to purchase fine clothes for himself. One description of Hercules has the slave wearing "white linen, black silk breeches and waistcoat, highly polished shoes with large buckles, a blue cloth coat with velvet collar and bright metal buttons, a watch fob and chain, cocked hat, and gold-headed cane."

Hercules is also famous for being one of the two slaves to escape from George Washington while in Philadelphia. When Washington moved to the President's House in Philadelphia, Pennsylvania was in the process of freeing its slaves. Because the state had passed a law saying that slaves residing in state would be considered free if they stayed more than six months, every six months Washington shipped his slaves home to Virginia and then immediately brought them back to restart the six-month clock.

When Washington's second term ended in March 1797 and the former president was packing up for Mount Vernon one final time, Hercules decided that the time was ripe for him to leave. He packed up his clothes and disappeared into Philadelphia, never to be seen again. Washington made a few weak efforts to find him, but Hercules had disappeared and became a free man.

Oney Judge, Personal Slave of Martha Washington. Another slave, Oney Judge, also used her time in the President's House in Philadelphia to escape from Washington's clutches. She is the best known of all the Mount Vernon slaves because after her escape, she was interviewed extensively by abolitionist newspapers because of her connection to President Washington and the means of her escape.

Oney Judge, the daughter of a black slave and a white indentured servant at Mount Vernon, was the personal slave of the president's wife, Martha Washington. Oney accompanied the Washingtons on shopping trips and other excursions, and the president and Mrs. Washington took her with them when they moved to both New York City and Philadelphia.

As Martha's personal slave, Oney would help Martha dress for official receptions; travel with her on social calls and outings; and execute daily errands. Despite her usefulness and longtime service to the Washingtons, Oney was told that she was going to be given to one of the Washingtons' great-grandchildren as a wedding gift. That was the final straw. Her chance to escape came in 1796 as the Washingtons were packing up in Philadelphia to spend some time at Mount Vernon. "Whilst they were packing up to go to Virginia, I was packing to go, I didn't know where; for I knew that if I went back to Virginia, I should never get my liberty," Oney Judge said in a interview in 1845. "I had friends among the colored people of Philadelphia, had my things carried there beforehand, and left Washington's house while they were eating dinner."

Oney's friends delivered her to a ship called the *Nancy*, and she sailed for Portsmouth, New Hampshire, where she stepped off the ship a free woman. However, she was not safe. Only days after Oney's arrival in Portsmouth, she was recognized by one of the Washingtons' friends, Elizabeth Langdon, the daughter of New Hampshire senator John Langdon. Langdon tried to talk to Oney, but the freed slave eluded her. Now Washington knew where she was though, and he was determined to get her back.

The ex-president enlisted the help of the collector of customs in Portsmouth, John Whipple, in his attempt to find Oney, and Whipple tracked her down. However, after talking to Oney and hearing about her desire for freedom, Whipple refused to arrest her and have her shipped south. He said he feared a riot on the docks from the abolitionist New Englanders.

Oney still was not safe though. Washington's nephew, Burnwell Bassett Jr., came up to New Hampshire on business and stayed with the Langdons, the same family that had informed the Washingtons of Oney's whereabouts. Bassett mentioned to them that while he was in New Hampshire, he hoped to track down Oney and take her and any children she might have back with him to Mount Vernon to return them to slavery. This time the Langdons decided to help the runaway slave. They quickly sent word to Oney that Bassett planned to kidnap her, and she fled Portsmouth for a neighboring town. There, she hid with a free black family until after Bassett had left. Three months after this incident, George Washington died, and Oney was free forever.

Asked later in her life if she ever missed her life at Mount Vernon and with the Washingtons, Oney said, "No, I am free, and have, I trust, been made a child of God by the means." Ona "Oney" Judge Staines died in Greenland, New Hampshire, on February 25, 1848.

Black Men Built the White House, Too

The building where the most powerful man in the world sleeps today has had black connections since before it was built. While Washington's slaves were the first black participants in the presidency, blacks were also deeply involved in the construction of the White House as we know it today.

The city planners originally planned to import workers from other cities and even from overseas to work on buildings like the White House, but they quickly realized that city commissioners were turning instead to slaves in Maryland and Virginia. In 1791, Pierre L'Enfant, with the permission of the city commissioners, hired slaves from their masters to help dig the foundation for the White House. According to *The Presidents' House, Vol. I,* by William Seale, "L'Enfant's laborers were Negro Slaves hired by the month from their masters. In the spring the commission resolved to employ thereafter 'good laboring negroes by the year.' The money was good, £21 per year; the commission agreed to provide food, while the master was to furnish clothing and a blanket for each man."

Quarrying stone. While the foundation was being dug, other slaves in Virginia were quarrying the stone that would be used for the walls of the White House. According to *The President's House,* in 1972 the city commission "had hired twenty-five able bodied negroe men slaves to be employed at the quarries." It is likely that more were hired later on to dig the freestone out of the quarry in Stafford County, Virginia, at Aquia Creek.

Master stonemason Collen Williamson trained slaves on the spot to quarry the rough stone. Slaves, using pickaxes, mauls, and wedges, chopped the stone out of the ground. Once the stone was freed from the ground in large slabs, it was dragged to a wharf where it would be shipped forty miles north to Washington. When the stone reached Washington, slaves were called upon again to transport it to the White House. According to Bob Arnebeck's 1991 book *Through a Fiery Trial: Building Washington 1790–1800,* "it took six slaves two days to unload one shallop load. And then it took eight slaves three days to put that load on the drags" to be taken to the White House.

Digging Clay and Sawing Timber. Many slaves dug up clay for the thousands of bricks that were needed for the White House, while others sawed the lumber the construction required. In May 1796 a man referred to as "Negro William" worked as a bricklayer earning $1.33 a day, equal to what white masons were getting. According to Arnebeck, at least twenty-one slaves cut timber for the White House, and they, or more likely their masters, got paid one shilling a day (13 cents). Some did better. Eight slaves received extra pay in August 1795 for their work as sawyers at the White House. One of them, Simon, was evidently skilled since he was paid almost $1 a day. The other seven slaves received 13 cents a day.

Construction and Carpentry. Slaves did not just work outside the White House. One of the earliest payrolls shows that at least five slave carpenters were at work inside the White House in January 1795, each making as little as 53 cents to as much as 84 cents a day for their masters. White carpenters made more than $1 a day.

James Hoban, the South Carolinian who won the design competition for the White House and was responsible for its construction, brought with him from the South at least four of the slaves who worked inside the White House. The wages that were paid for the work of Peter, Ben, Harry, and Daniel inside the White House, equaling about $60 for the month, went to Hoban.

Slaves were not the only blacks to work on the White House. Free blacks also worked there, as evidenced by the story of Jerry Holland. He was one of nine laborers working on a surveying crew at the White House, and in January 1795 he was praised in writing by one of his supervisors: "Pay Jerry the black man a rate of $8 per month for his last months services; he is justly entitled to the highest wages that is due to our hands—being promised it and the best hand in the department."

African Americans at the White House

The black contribution to the presidency did not end with the construction of the White House. The second child ever born at the White House was black. The first was Thomas Jefferson's grandson, Thomas Jefferson Randolph. But the second was the child of two of Jefferson's White House slaves, Fanny and Eddy. Unfortunately, the child only lived two years past its birth in 1806, but if it had lived, it would have joined the legions of slaves that worked in the White House in the early days of the presidency. While Jefferson and other pre–Civil War presidents were shaping this country, blacks were running the President's House and making sure that the president was well taken care of.

Starting with Jefferson's administration, the majority of the White House staff from 1800 through the Civil War consisted of slaves. These slaves went with the U.S. presidents to work in the White House because at that time Congress did not provide money for a domestic staff for the president. Presidents who owned slaves—Thomas Jefferson, James Madison, Andrew Jackson, John Tyler, James Polk, and Zachary Taylor—brought them to the White House where they formed the core of the White House domestic staff and lived on what is now considered to be the ground floor.

James Hemings, First White House Chef—Almost

Thomas Jefferson wanted the first White House chef to be a black, and a free one at that. Before becoming president, Jefferson spent time in France, taking with him a nineteen-year-old slave named James Hemings. The slave, who was the older brother of Jefferson's mistress Sally Hemings, spent the next three years learning from the finest French caterers and cooks and became Jefferson's main cook while he was in Paris. Once back in America, James Hemings asked Jefferson for his freedom. The future president consented, but only if Hemings would train another slave to cook in his place.

Hemings did as he was asked and was freed by Jefferson. However, by 1801, Thomas Jefferson had become president, and he wanted Hemings back. The new president contacted the now-free Hemings and tried to convince him to come to Washington to use his French culinary training as the first White House chef. Hemings said no, perhaps preferring the traveling he did after leaving Jefferson's household. Jefferson hired a white man named Julian as chef, and Hemings's refusal to serve as White House chef resulted in a Jefferson White House domestic staff that was almost all black and almost all slave—except for chief steward and chef.

Paul Jennings, Slave of James Madison and Daniel Webster

One of James Madison's slaves is credited with a historic first; he became the first White House employee to write a tell-all book about life in the White House. This slave was named Paul Jennings, and his 1865 book is called *A Colored Man's Reminiscences of James Madison.*

Jennings, who was Madison's personal slave and stayed with him until Madison died, used his book to tell stories of the War of 1812 and the burning of the White House. It is because of Jennings that we know that Dolly Madison did not grab a painting of George Washington as she and the White House staff fled invading British troops, as is often said. It is also because of Jennings that the world knows that blacks served not only in the Revolutionary War, but in the War of 1812 as well. Jennings describes one group of sailors-turned-soldiers who were trying to hold off the invading British in Bladensburg, Maryland:

> Commander Barney's flotilla was stripped of men, who were placed in battery, at Bladensburg, where they fought splendidly. A large part of his men were tall, strapping Negroes, mixed with white sailors and marines. Mr. Madison reviewed them just before the fight, and asked Commander Barney if his "Negroes would not run on the approach of the British?"
>
> "No sir," said Barney, "they don't know how to run; they will die by their guns first."
>
> They fought till a large part of them were killed or wounded; and Barney himself wounded and taken prisoner.

Jennings's final contribution came after the death of President Madison. Madison died penniless, leaving Dolly Madison to depend on charity to survive. Meanwhile, Jennings was working toward his freedom. Dolly Madison sold Jennings for $200, and the famous Senator Daniel Webster of Massachusetts bought him later for a mere $120. Webster promised to free Jennings after he worked off the money that was spent to purchase him, but Jennings took time away from his quest for freedom to help Mrs. Madison.

Jennings wrote:

> In the last days of her life, before Congress purchased her husband's papers, she was in a state of absolute poverty, and I think sometimes suffered for the necessaries of life. While I was a servant to Mr. Webster, he often sent me to her with a market-basket full of provisions, and told me whenever I saw anything in the house that I thought she was in need of, to take it to her. I often did this, and occasionally gave her small sums from my own pocket, though I had years before bought my freedom of her.

While working for Webster, Jennings also played a key role in the greatest mass escape attempt by slaves in American history. Despite being owned his entire life by kindly masters like the Madisons and Webster, Jennings felt that slavery was wrong for both him and the other enslaved blacks in the Washing-ton, D.C., area. After he met a ship captain named Daniel Drayton of Philadel-phia in 1848, he and Drayton hatched a plot to spirit away as many slaves from the nation's capital as possible. Aided by free black families in the area, Jennings, Drayton, and another sea captain named Edmund Sayres spread the news that freedom was available if slaves were courageous enough to try to seek it.

A few days later, more than seventy men, women, and children snuck aboard the *Pearl*, a borrowed schooner sitting in a Washington wharf. In addi-tion to the slaves aboard the ship, several free black families came along to help their enslaved relatives and brethren.

Before heading for the ship, Jennings took time to write a letter to Senator Webster and left it for the out-of-town politician to find later.

> A deep desire to be of help to my poor people has determined me to take a decided step in that direction. My only regret is that I shall appear ungrateful, in thus leaving with so little ceremony, one who has been uni-formly kind and considerate and had rendered each moment of service a benefaction as well as pleasure. From the daily contact with your great per-sonality which it has been mine to enjoy, has been imbibed a respect for moral obligations and the claims of duty. Both of these draw me towards the path I have chosen.

However, just before the *Pearl* set sail, Jennings changed his mind. He had entered into an agreement with Webster and felt that his honor was at stake if he broke his word by escaping to freedom. He said his good-byes to his friends aboard the *Pearl* and returned to Webster's house, where he retrieved his letter.

Jennings was lucky he stayed ashore. The *Pearl* headed down the Potomac and made it as far as Point Lookout, Maryland, where the Potomac meets the Chesapeake Bay. But there the winds died, leaving the schooner dead in the water less than 150 miles away from the nation's capital. Meanwhile, the angry slave masters were on the hunt, but the escape was so well planned that they didn't know which way the escaped slaves went.

However, according to Josephine F. Pacheco in *The Pearl*, the slaves were betrayed by one of their own. A black man named Judson Diggs supposedly revealed the plan because one of the escaped slaves did not pay him for hauling his belongings down to the ship with his horse and wagon. The slave owners jumped on a steamer and raced after the *Pearl*, still adrift in windless water.

After being returned to Washington in chains, most of the African Americans on the ship, whether escaped slave or free black family, were immediately put up on the auction block for sale to the Deep South. The whites onboard were jailed, and Drayton was not released until he received a presidential pardon four years later in 1852.

Jennings, meanwhile, evaded blame in the escape. He made it back to Webster's house and retrieved the letter he had written, so no one connected him to the *Pearl.* He didn't forget the people he had tried to help, however. He was one of the main fund-raisers who worked to save at least one of the *Pearl* families from being sold into slavery.

Elizabeth Keckley, Seamstress for the Lincolns

A second African American also wrote a tell-all book about the White House and the presidency after spending a considerable amount of time on the inside. The book, called *Thirty Years a Slave and Four Years in the White House,* was written by a freedwoman named Elizabeth Keckley in 1868. She was a seamstress who came to the attention of Abraham Lincoln and his wife Mary Todd

Elizabeth Keckley

Lincoln because of her skill as a dressmaker.

After being hired by Mrs. Lincoln to make a dress, Elizabeth Keckley became the first lady's best friend and spent many hours inside the White House with President Lincoln and his wife. The Lincolns so trusted Keckley that the president would ask her to comb his hair and make him presentable before leaving the White House. "When almost ready to go down to a reception, he would turn to me with a quizzical look: 'Well, Madam Elizabeth, will you brush my bristles down to-night?'" Keckley wrote in her book. Keckley wrote that she would reply, "'Yes, Mr. Lincoln.' Then he would take his seat in an easy-chair, and sit quietly while I arranged his hair."

Mrs. Lincoln and Elizabeth Keckley were so close that on the night Lincoln was assassinated, the president's wife wanted only Keckley for company. Keckley wrote in her book, "I afterwards learned, that when she had partially recovered from the first shock of the terrible tragedy in the theatre, Mrs. Welles asked: 'Is there no one, Mrs. Lincoln that you desire to have with you in this terrible affliction?'" According to Keckley, Mrs. Lincoln answered, "Yes, send for Elizabeth Keckley. I want her just as soon as she can be brought here." Keckley stayed with Mrs. Lincoln through the funeral and during her transition out of the White House. She wrote:

> Mrs. Lincoln never left her room, and while the body of her husband was being borne in solemn state from the Atlantic to the broad prairies of the West, she was weeping with her fatherless children in her private chamber. She denied admittance to almost every one, and I was her only companion, except her children, in the days of her great sorrow.

Keckley's book reveals several secrets that Mrs. Lincoln would have preferred to have kept quiet, including Mrs. Lincoln's flirtation with Lincoln's rival, Stephen Douglas; the massive debt the first lady left behind as a result of her shopping trips in Washington; the illiteracy of the Lincolns' youngest son; and Mrs. Lincoln's attempt to sell her wardrobe to raise money post–White House. Consequently, the remaining Lincolns shunned Keckley for the rest of her life and attempted to have her book banned.

Keckley earned her living by sewing, and she received a small pension for her son's death in the Civil War. She eventually went to work for Wilberforce College, the nation's oldest historically black private university.

Famous Black Visitors to the White House

Although African Americans have always been present inside the White House in some capacity, it took years for the first African-American man and woman to be formally received inside the president's mansion.

Frederick Douglass. The first African-American leader to have a formal meeting with the president inside the White House was Frederick Douglass, who met with President Lincoln in July 1863 about the treatment of black soldiers in the Union Army. Douglass, who had two sons serve with the famed 54th Massachusetts Regiment, asked Lincoln to make sure that black troops got paid the same as white troops. He also asked that they be treated fairly if captured by the Confederates instead of being summarily executed and that they receive the same promotions as whites. Lincoln later issued a proclamation stating that for any

African-American Firsts at the White House

1859. Thomas Green Bethune, nicknamed "Blind Tom," became the first black musician to perform at the White House. Blind Tom, considered to be one of the greatest musical prodigies of his day, played piano for President James Buchanan.

1866. William Slade was a former Treasury Department messenger who became President Lincoln's personal messenger and friend. After Lincoln's assassination, Slade was appointed the first White House steward for Lincoln's successor, President Andrew Johnson, in August 1866. Slade was the first person, black or white, to hold this official position. As White House steward, Slade was in charge of running the domestic side of the White House, and he was responsible for the furniture, paintings, silver, and other public property. Slade died during Johnson's term in office.

1878. Soprano **Marie Seilka** became the first black singer to perform at the White House when she sang for President Rutherford B. Hayes.

1911. William Henry Lewis was the first African American appointed by a president (William Howard Taft) to a White House sub-Cabinet post: assistant attorney general.

1936. Mary McLeod Bethune was appointed director of the division of Minority Affairs of the National Youth Administration, a New Deal agency, by President Franklin Roosevelt. This was the first presidential appointment giving an African American a leadership position in an executive agency.

"United States soldier [black or white] killed in violation of the laws of war, a rebel soldier would be executed; and for every one enslaved by the enemy or sold into slavery, a rebel soldier shall be placed at hard labour on the public works."

Sojourner Truth. Sojourner Truth was likely the first African-American woman to be formally received in the White House. Truth, who was living at the time in

1955. E. Frederick Morrow, an administrative assistant for President Dwight Eisenhower, was the first black to be officially appointed a White House aide. He wrote *Black Man in the White House* before becoming the first black corporate executive (for Bank of America) in 1964.

1960. Andrew T. Hatcher was the first African American to be named associate White House press secretary. He served in this position for President John F. Kennedy.

1993. Sharon Farmer was named chief White House photographer, one of the photography world's most prestigious positions. She was the first black female to become a White House photographer. The first black White House photographer, Ricardo Thomas, had been hired during the Ford administration.

1996. *Sand Dunes at Sunset, Atlantic City,* a painting by **Henry Ossawa Tanner,** was the first painting by an African-American artist to be added to the White House's permanent collection. It hangs in the Green Room of the White House. Tanner was the first African-American artist to gain international fame and was the most renowned African-American artist of the nineteenth century.

2004. With his oil painting of President Bill Clinton, **Simmie Knox** was the first African-American artist to paint an official White House presidential portrait. He also painted a White House portrait of First Lady (and future New York senator) Hillary Rodham Clinton.

a black village located at the current site of Arlington National Cemetery, met with Lincoln in the White House on October 29, 1864. Her meeting with the president was arranged by Elizabeth Keckley and a white abolitionist named Lucy Colman. Because she was illiterate, Truth later dictated what happened in that meeting for a letter that was published in her 1850 book, *The Narrative of Sojourner Truth: A Northern Slave:*

> It was about 8 o'clock a.m., when I called on the president. Upon entering his reception room we found about a dozen persons in waiting, among them two colored women. I had quite a pleasant time waiting until he was disengaged, and enjoying his conversation with others; he showed as much kindness and consideration to the colored persons as to the whites—if there was any difference, more. One case was that of a colored woman who was sick and likely to be turned out of her house on account of her inability to pay her rent. The president listened to her with much attention, and spoke to her with kindness and tenderness. He said he had given so much he could give no more, but told her where to go and get the money, and asked Mrs. C—n to assist her, which she did. . . .
>
> I said to him, Mr. President, when you first took your seat I feared you would be torn to pieces, for I likened you unto Daniel, who was thrown into the lion's den; and if the lions did not tear you into pieces, I knew that it would be God that had saved you; and I said, if he spared me I would see you before the four years expired, and he has done so, and now I am here to see you for myself. . . .
>
> He then congratulated me upon having been spared. Then I said, I appreciate you, for you are the best president who has ever taken the seat. He replied: "I expect you have reference to my having emancipated the slaves in my proclamation. But," said he, mentioning the names of several of his predecessors (and among them emphatically that of Washington), "they were all just as good, and would have done just as I have done if the time had come. If the people over the river [pointing across the Potomac] had behaved themselves, I could not have done what I have; but they did not, which gave the opportunity to do those things." I then said, I thank God that you were the instrument selected by him and the people to do it.

Truth apparently was not intimidated by meeting the president in his office, because the next thing she said to Lincoln was that she had never heard of him before he became president. Truth's account has Lincoln grinning at her remark and replying, "I had heard of you many times before that."

A commissioned painting records this meeting between Lincoln and Truth, depicting the president and the abolitionist looking at the Lincoln Bible, an ornate Bible presented to the president by African Americans in Baltimore. In Truth's letter, she says that Lincoln showed her the Bible, which she found to be "beautiful beyond description."

Sojourner Truth and Abraham Lincoln examining a Bible in the White House
LIBRARY OF CONGRESS, LC-USZ62-16225

> After I had looked it over, I said to him, This is beautiful indeed; the colored people have given this to the head of the government, and that government once sanctioned laws that would not permit its people to learn enough to enable them to read this book. And for what? Let them answer who can.

Truth said she was pleased with her reception at the White House and even came away with a souvenir.

> I must say, and I am proud to say, that I never was treated by any one with more kindness and cordiality than were shown to me by that great and good man, Abraham Lincoln, by the grace of God president of the United States for four years more. He took my little book, and with the same hand that signed the death-warrant of slavery, wrote as follows "For Aunty Sojourner Truth, Oct. 29, 1864. A. Lincoln."

DISCOVERING BLACK HISTORY IN THE REST OF WASHINGTON, D.C.

Washington, D.C., is divided into four quadrants: Northeast, Northwest, Southeast, and Southwest.

Northeast

Northeast is largely residential, but there are several sites worth seeing in this area while in town.

The National Capitol Columns at the United States National Arboretum

For plant lovers, the United States National Arboretum would be worth seeing even if it didn't have an African-American history connection: 446 acres and 9 miles of roadways connect numerous gardens and collections, including the National Grove of State Trees, National Herb Garden, Dogwood Collection, Fern Valley, Holly and Magnolia Collection, and National Bonsai and Penjing Museum.

But near the center of this wonderful campus is one of Washington's most unique monuments, the National Capitol Columns. These magnificent columns are one of the few things that people can actually touch in the United States capital that were once touched by slaves, and they are worth the trip for that reason alone. The twenty-five-ton columns began their life as part of the East Portico of the Capitol in 1828. But they were dismantled and removed from the

Capitol in 1958 in favor of marble reconstructions to ensure that the weight of the Capitol dome was adequately supported. The dismantled columns languished in several spots around Washington, D.C., for years until they were reinstalled at the arboretum in 1984.

These majestic columns would not exist if not for slave labor in Virginia. The sandstone the columns were carved from came from an area near Aquia Creek in Virginia. Aquia Creek was a quarry that was staffed by slaves. In 1792 Washington's city commissioners authorized hiring as many as forty slaves at Aquia Creek at $32 a year plus provisions. The commissioners promised to provide housing and provisions while the slaves' masters were to provide clothing and a blanket.

The slaves quarried sandstone at the Aquia quarries six days a week, from sunup to sundown. The stone was hauled to small ships that sailed down the Potomac to Washington harbor, and then it was hauled by more slaves to the Capitol. There, slaves assisted stonecutters in carving the Capitol columns.

Frederick Douglass Museum and Hall of Fame for Caring Americans

Although famed orator and statesman Frederick Douglass lived and worked in Rochester, New York, for the majority of his adult life, he lived out the last few decades of his life in homes in Washington, D.C. The Frederick Douglass Museum and Hall of Fame for Caring Americans in Capitol Hill is the location of Douglass's first home in the District of Columbia.

One reason Douglass moved from New York State to the District of Columbia was because his home in New York burned to the ground, destroying many of his papers and the valuable early editions of the *North Star*. Arson was suspected, but no one was ever arrested. After this loss, Douglass decided not to rebuild in Rochester and moved his family into a town house at 314 A Street NE in Washington, D.C, where he spent roughly seven years (1872–1878) living only blocks from the U.S. Capitol. Douglass began a new era in his life from this house—an era of trailblazing government service as the nation's top civil rights orator.

Douglass came to D.C. to work as publisher for the *New Era,* a weekly paper established in the area to serve former slaves. He renamed the paper the *New National Era* and published it until it shut down in 1874.

He also dabbled in finance, becoming the president of the national Freedman's Bank in 1874. The Freedman's Bank was created to provide financial services for blacks drafted during the Civil War, and its headquarters was located in Washington, D.C. Douglass had high hopes when he took the position. "When I came to Washington and saw its magnificent brown stone front, its towering height, and its perfect appointments, and the fine display it made in the transaction of its business, I felt like the Queen of Sheba when she saw the riches of Solomon," he wrote in his final autobiography, *The Life and Times of Frederick Douglass.* But his presence was not enough to save the bank, which suffered from risky loan policies and from fraud and mismanagement by poorly trained white administrators. Douglass wrote in the 1881 book:

> The fact is, and all investigation shows it, that I was married to a corpse. The fine building was there with its marble counters and black walnut finishings, the affable and agile clerks, and the discreet and comely colored cashier; but the LIFE, which was the money, was gone, and I found that I had been placed there with the hope that by "some drugs, some charms, some conjuration, or some mighty magic," I would bring it back.

The national Freedman's Bank and all its branches collapsed in 1874, and Douglass was forced to ask Congress to liquidate all remaining assets. Douglass called his involvement with the Freedman's Bank an event "which has brought upon my head an amount of abuse and detraction greater than any encountered in any other part of my life." The failure of the *New National Era* and the Freedman's Bank did not tarnish Douglass's reputation completely, however. He managed to accomplish some historic firsts while living in Capitol Hill.

In 1872, Douglass became the first African American to be nominated for vice president. Without his knowledge, he was nominated to be Victoria Woodhull's running mate on the Equal Rights Party ticket. During the campaign, he neither campaigned for the ticket nor acknowledged that he had been nominated.

Douglass also became the first African American to be successfully confirmed by the Senate to a government position. In 1877 President Rutherford B. Hayes nominated him to be U.S. marshal of the District of Columbia. Douglass himself understood the historic importance of the appointment. In a March 21, 1877, letter to Samuel Drummond Porter, he wrote: "Only men like yourself, men born in advance of their time, men who knew and comprehended the dignity of human nature, whether under one complexion or another, long before these sunny days, can now fully comprehend the significance of this appointment and confirmation."

Despite the historical significance of being appointed D.C.'s marshal, this was not Douglass's first opportunity to work for the government. In July 1867 Douglass was asked by President Andrew Johnson to take charge of the Freedman's Bureau, which would have put him in control of all government programs for freed southern blacks. It was the first time a major government post had been offered to an African American, but Douglass turned it down. Douglass refused the position because it would have associated his name with President Johnson, who had told Douglass and other African-American leaders that he intended to support the interests of southern whites and block voting rights for blacks.

In addition to the aforementioned accomplishments, Douglass made several other achievements while he was living in Washington, D.C. President James Garfield named him the District of Columbia recorder of deeds; President Benjamin Harrison selected him to be the United States' minister to Haiti; and President Ulysses S. Grant made him secretary of the commission of Santo Domingo.

The Frederick Douglass Museum and Hall of Fame for Caring Americans has mementoes and memorabilia from Douglass's time in Capitol Hill and has restored Douglass's town house to its nineteenth-century splendor. It also hosts exhibits about people who have received the National Caring Award from the Caring Institute, administered separately by the same organization.

The First Museum of African Art. Frederick Douglass's town house was also the location of the first national museum of African art. The museum was eventually taken over by the Smithsonian Institution and moved to its current location on the National Mall.

Union Station: A. Philip Randolph Memorial Bust

Union Station is a major crossroads for people visiting the District of Columbia. From this hub, visitors can rent a car, hail a taxi, catch a bus, ride the subway, or catch one of the many Amtrak trains that runs up and down the eastern seaboard. It's appropriate, then, that Union Station is the location for a memorial to one of the pioneers of the African-American civil rights and labor rights movement, A. Philip Randolph. Randolph is best known as the founder and president of the Brotherhood of Sleeping Car Porters, but he was also was the chair of the famous 1963 March on Washington for Jobs and Freedom.

The bronze statue of A. Philip Randolph (the "A." in his name stands for Asa) was created by African-American sculptor Ed Dwight and was donated to Union Station by the American Federation of Labor-Congress of Industrial Unions (AFL-CIO) in 1990. Randolph stands watching over the arriving and departing train passengers, just as he watched over working minorities and the poor during his long life as a journalist and labor and civil rights activist.

Basilica of the National Shrine of the Immaculate Conception, Mother of Africa Shrine

The Basilica of the National Shrine of the Immaculate Conception in Northeast D.C. is the largest Catholic church in the Western Hemisphere, as well as one of the largest churches of any denomination in the world. (It is the third-largest church in the United States, following only the Cathedral of St. John the Divine in New York City and the Cathedral Church of St. Peter and St. Paul, better known as the Washington National Cathedral.)

Comprised of an Upper Church and a Crypt Church, the National Shrine is so large that the Statue of Liberty could easily fit lengthwise in the Upper Church. Dedicated in 1959, the National Shrine measures 459 feet long and covers an area of 77,500 square feet.

Located in the northeast quadrant of Washington on land donated by the Catholic University of America, the National Shrine is designated as a National Historic Landmark on the National Register of Historic Places. It is also the pre-eminent Marian Shrine and Patronal Catholic Church of the United States, honoring Mary, Mother of God, under the title Immaculate Conception.

Deep inside the Crypt Church sits the Our Mother of Africa Chapel, a gift to the National Shrine from African-American Catholics under the leadership of the National Black Catholic Congress and the Black Bishops of the United States. It is the first chapel in the National Shrine dedicated to African Americans. Dedicated on August 30, 1997, and paid for solely through donations, Our Mother of Africa Chapel features at its threshold a marble inlay showing the *Henrietta Marie,* a slave ship that sank near Key West, Florida, in the early 1700s

A. Philip Randolph, Early Civil Rights Leader

A. Philip Randolph was born in Crescent City, Florida, on April 15, 1889. In 1925 Randolph became president of the first predominantly black labor union,

the Brotherhood of Sleeping Car Porters, whose goal was to improve working conditions for the nearly ten thousand black railroad employees of the Pullman Company, a major African-American employer at the time.

After dealing with years of union-busting tactics and neglect from other labor unions (many affiliates of the American Federation of Labor barred African Americans from membership at the time), the Brotherhood finally got the Pullman Company to negotiate with them in 1935. The company signed a contract with the Brotherhood in 1937, marking the first time a contract was ever drawn up between a company and a black union.

Randolph's work in civil rights was just as groundbreaking as his work for labor. Randolph, the chair of the 1963 March on Washington for Jobs and Freedom, had originally planned for the March on Washington to be held more than two decades earlier, in 1941.

Randolph saw the ramping up of America's economy for World War II through the building of new factories and new plants to support the armed forces. However, around the country, African Americans were systematically being denied employment in these factories. And the same federal government that was preparing to send African Americans overseas in segregated units to fight for their country was offering no redress or help.

In 1941 Randolph threatened to bring ten thousand African American men to Washington, D.C., to protest discrimination in the wartime workplace. Before long, ten thousand men turned into one hundred thousand men and women, ready and eager to march on Washington.

Seeing a major demonstration preparing to march on his doorstep, President Franklin Roosevelt felt he had no choice. On June 25, 1941, he issued Executive Order 8802, barring discrimination in defense industries and federal bureaus and creating the Fair Employment Practices Committee to enforce that decree. This was the very first executive order protecting African-American rights since the Emancipation Proclamation. Once Roosevelt issued the executive order, Randolph called off the march, angering many of the young radicals who wanted to march on the federal government.

A. Philip Randolph
LIBRARY OF CONGRESS, LC-USW3-011696-C

After World War II ended, Randolph looked at the segregated military and demanded that the new president, Harry S. Truman, end the policies of discrimination in the armed services. On June 26, 1948, Randolph formed a new group, the League for Non-Violent Civil Disobedience against Military Segregation. Three days later, he met with President Truman and warned him that if he didn't issue an executive order ending segregation in the armed forces, African-American youth would resist the draft law.

A month after the formation of the League for Non-Violent Civil Disobedience against Military Segregation, President Truman signed Executive Order 9981, which states, "It is hereby declared to be the policy of the President that there shall be equality of treatment and opportunity for all persons in the armed services without regard to race, color, religion, or national origin."

Randolph was named the official chair of the 1963 March on Washington for Jobs and Freedom, even though the economic focus that Randolph wanted was pushed slightly to the wayside for civil rights concerns.

A. Philip Randolph died on May 16, 1979, in New York City.

after delivering a consignment of African captives to the island of Jamaica.

Inside the chapel, a mahogany vaulted ceiling reminds visitors of the hulls of seaborne vessels, while a bronze statue of Our Mother of Africa holding the Christ child awaits visitors. Created by African-American sculptor Ed Dwight, the eight-foot Mother of Africa strides forward toward a narrative bas-relief in the chapel showing the history of African Americans and the Catholic Church. In her arms her divine son gestures for us to read the relief, which spans the African-American experience from slavery to emancipation. Both figures have been carved with idealized African-American features.

At the far end of the relief is an altar with a crucifix bearing a black Christ on a carved cross, the work of Juvenal Kaliki, a Tanzanian sculptor from the Entebene tribe, and New York sculptor Jeffrey Brosk. Kaliki carved the Christ in a carving tradition that dates back five centuries in his Entebene tribe, using a black hardwood called ebony. Brosk, meanwhile, hewed his cross from cherry wood, retaining the natural curves of the tree and the bark's irregular surface.

The chapel also features sculptures of the four New Testament evangelists—Matthew, Mark, Luke, and John—each carved in gray Bardiglio marble with distinct African features.

The Supreme Court

Decisions made by justices at the Supreme Court building next to the U.S. Capitol profoundly affect African-American life in America today, as they have for hundreds of years. But the familiar building sitting next to the U.S. Capitol has not always been the home of the supreme judicial branch of the United States. For years the Supreme Court shared space with Congress inside the Capitol, and the Court didn't get its own building at the corner of East Capitol and First Street NE until 1935.

Despite its early nomadic existence, the Supreme Court's effect on African Americans cannot be underestimated. Since 1857, when an all-white court ruled in *Dred Scott v. Sanford* that African Americans were not entitled to the same rights as white citizens, African Americans have worked through the Court to demand the rights of full citizenship.

Dr. John Sweat Rock. African Americans have been challenging laws before the Supreme Court since the 1800s. The very first African-American lawyer

The Supreme Court

licensed to practice before the Supreme Court was Dr. John Sweat Rock, who was made part of the Supreme Court bar on February 1, 1865. Rock, who was born free in New Jersey, was a true Renaissance man. He was a teacher, doctor, and dentist by age twenty-seven, and he was good at what he did. He was given the honor of being one of the first African Americans admitted to the Massachusetts Medical Society, and he was one of the people to give medical aid to fugitive slaves as they passed through Boston on the Underground Railroad.

But he wasn't satisfied with that, adding to his resume experience as a politician, lecturer, lawyer, justice of the peace, and military recruiter for the 54th Massachusetts. The capstone on his resume, however, came in 1865, when he was admitted to the Supreme Court bar. He found an advocate in Washington, D.C., Senator Charles Sumner of Massachusetts, who helped convince Chief Justice Solomon Chase to admit an African-American lawyer. The *New York Tribune* covered the momentous occasion.

Key Supreme Court Decisions Affecting African-American Civil Rights

1857. *Dred Scott v. Sanford*. Ruled that African Americans were not citizens entitled to the full rights and privileges of white citizens.

 1896. *Plessy v. Ferguson*. The famous "separate but equal" decision declared that segregation was legal and constitutional as long as "facilities were equal."

1954. *Brown v. Board of Education of Topeka, Kansas*. Reversed the *Plessy v. Ferguson* "separate but equal" ruling.

1967. *Loving v. Virginia*. Banned prohibitions on interracial marriage.

2003. *Grutter v. Bollinger*. Upheld affirmative action in education as long it employed a "highly individualized, holistic review of each applicant's file" and did not consider race as a factor in a "mechanical way."

At three minutes before eleven o'clock in the morning, Charles Sumner entered the Courtroom, followed by the negro [sic] applicant for admission, and sat down within the bar. At eleven, the procession of gowned judges entered the room, with Chief Justice Chase at their head. The spectators and their lawyers in attendance rose respectfully on their coming. The Associate Justices seated themselves nearly at once, as is their courteous custom of waiting upon each other's movements. The Chief Justice, standing to the last, bowed with affable dignity to the Bar, and took his central seat with a great presence. Immediately the Senator from Massachusetts arose, and in composed manner and quiet tone said: "May it please the Court, I move that John S. Rock, a member of the Supreme Court of the State of Massachusetts, be admitted to practice as a member of this Court." The grave to bury the Dred Scott decision was in that one sentence dug; and it yawned there, wide open, under the very eyes of some of the Judges who had participated in the judicial crime against Democracy and humanity. The assenting nod of the great head of the Chief Justice tumbled in course and filled up the pit, and the black counsellor of the Supreme Court got on to it and stamped it down and smoothed the earth to his walk to the rolls of the Court.

Dr. John Sweat Rock's position as the first African-American lawyer admitted to the Supreme Court bar opened other doors for him. Credited with coining the phrase "Black is beautiful," Rock was also one of the first African Americans to be invited to the House of Representatives and received on the House floor. He died in 1866, before he had a chance to argue a case in the Supreme Court.

The Old Brick Capitol and the Old Capitol Prison

African-American history does not end with the work inside the Supreme Court building. The site where the Supreme Court building now sits also has significant connections to African Americans. That location, at the corner of East Capitol and First Street NE, used to be the site of the Old Brick Capitol and, after that, the Old Capitol Prison.

The building that became the Old Brick Capitol was erected around 1800 as a tavern and boardinghouse. After the burning of the U.S. Capitol, there was some talk about moving the Capitol to another city. Instead, on December 8, 1815, Congress leased the Old Brick Capitol building for its own use. Two years later, in 1817, President James Monroe was inaugurated on a platform outside the building.

When Congress moved back into the U.S. Capitol in 1819, the Old Brick Capitol was used for various purposes until the Civil War. During that conflict, it became one of the era's most famous prisons. The Old Brick Capitol, now referred to as the Old Capitol Prison, was where the Union Army sent Confederate spies, saboteurs, and prisoners of war, as well as some Union soldiers who had run afoul of their own rules and regulations. Some famous prisoners of the Old Capitol Prison were female Confederate spies Belle Boyd and Rose O'Neal; Confederate Capt. Henry Wirz, commander of the infamous Andersonville prison in Georgia; and the Lincoln assassination conspirators.

The Old Capitol Prison was not just a federal government holding site; it was also an execution site. Quite a few people were hanged there: spies, political prisoners, and war criminals. Wirz was hanged at the Old Capitol for the poor treatment of Union soldiers at Andersonville; he was the only Confederate tried and hanged for war crimes. Also hanged on this site were four of the Lincoln assassination conspirators, including Mary Surratt, the first woman ever executed by the United States.

The Old Brick Capitol plaque on the Supreme Court steps

African Americans, both free and slave, also were present inside the Old Capitol Prison. Based on the writings of those who were eventually released from the Old Capitol Prison, we know that some African Americans worked there. One of the inmates, Virginia Lomax, wrote of an encounter with an African-American employee in her 1867 book *The Old Capitol and Its Inmates*:

> At this moment a negro woman entered, with a brass candlestick, three matches, and a piece of candle, which she put on the table, and taking the bedding from the floor, proceeded to spread it.
>
> "Do you know which is Mrs. Windsor's room?" I asked.
> "Yes; No. 10," she replied.
> "Mr. Nelson says I can get a towel from her. Will you ask her, if you please? Tell her it is for her cousin."
>
> The woman made no answer, but went on with her work as if she had not heard me.

The Old Capitol Prison LIBRARY OF CONGRESS LC-DIG-cwpb-00493

African Americans were also held as prisoners inside the Old Capitol Prison. With the availability of work in the still-under-construction nation's capital and the presence of a large free African-American population, the District of Columbia was an attractive destination for runaway slaves. But that didn't mean the city was a haven for African Americans.

Slave trading was prevalent in the District of Columbia during this era, and it was fully accepted by the local government. For example, when slave pens were full, businessmen opened private jails in locations like Seventh Street SW (where the Hirshhorn Museum is today), and Miller's Tavern, at 13th and F Street NW. The slave trade was so lucrative that even the private jails were eventually filled to capacity. That didn't stop slave owners from engaging in the trade. According to *Washington, City and Capital* by the Federal Writers' Project, "since the slave jails, colloquially known as 'Georgia pens,' and described by an ex-slave as worse than hog holes, were inadequate for the great demand, the public jails were made use of, accommodations for the criminals having to wait upon the more pressing and lucrative traffic in slaves."

Once the Civil War was in full swing, however, the slave prisons were closed, and the city of Washington had to solve the question of what to do with all of the now-free slaves (called "contraband" by the Union Army) who were heading toward the nation's capital. One solution they came up with was to send them to the Old Capitol Prison. Patricia C. Click mentions this solution in her 2001 book *Time Full of Trial: The Roanoke Island Freedmen's Colony, 1862–1867:*

> General Joseph K. F. Mansfield, commander of the Department of Washington, sent many of the new arrivals to a camp that had been organized at the Old Capitol Prison. The camp's superintendent found them jobs working for the military or private employers. When that location proved unsatisfactory, in part because some whites objected to housing the former slaves near white prisoners, the contrabands were moved to an area of tenements east of the Capitol known as Duff Green's Row.

We see another mention of this in the 1867 pamphlet *Addresses and Ceremonies at the New Year's Festival to the Freedmen, On Arlington Heights; And Statistics And Statements of the Educational Condition of the Colored People in the Southern States, And Other Facts,* found in *Pamphlets from the Daniel A. P. Murray Collection, 1818–1907* at the Library of Congress:

> In the opening of the war, a large number of fugitive slaves, from Maryland and Virginia, coming within our lines, made Washington their city of refuge. These colored people, then called "contrabands of war," were taken under the care of the Government. Their first home was in the Old Capitol, in which the first Congress that met in Washington city, in 1800, held its sessions, and which was used during the war as a place of confinement for rebel prisoners. Subsequently the quarters of these colored persons were located in "Duff Green's Row," a block of buildings on the same square, east of the present Capitol. These buildings have memorable associations connected with many of the leading men of the rebellion. John C. Calhoun, the father of secessionism, and the great champion of slavery in Congress, and other leading southerners, enjoyed the intimate hospitalities of the owner, whose name the buildings bear, and in them were held frequent social and political conferences during the reign of slavery.

Duff Green's Row. Duff Green's Row was a row of houses adjoining the Old Capitol Prison that was also used as part of the prison. According to the Friday, May 30, 1862, edition of *The Washington Star:*

> The contrabands—The slaves who have been escaping from their masters in Maryland and Virginia and who have received the title of the Contrabands, are mostly quartered in Duff Green's Row on Capitol Hill, where

Miller's Tavern Was Actually a Slave Prison

MORE FACTS

Behind the deceptive name "Miller's Tavern" was in reality one of the District's worst slave prisons. According to "Washington, City and Capital" by the Federal Writers' Project, a New Deal program which was published by the U. S. Government Printing Office in 1937 in the District of Columbia:

[When] Miller's Tavern at Thirteenth and F Streets NW was on fire, a bystander, William Gardiner, refused to join the customary bucket brigade and loudly denounced the place as a slave prison. The resulting controversy conducted in newspaper columns revealed the tragic past of the tavern. A Negro woman about to be sold South apart from her husband, had leapt in frenzy from an attic window, breaking both arms and injuring her back, but surviving. This focused attention upon the local slave trade. Humanitarian Jesse Torrey came to Washington shortly after the attempted suicide, visited the injured woman and discovered two kidnapped Negroes in the attic. He began a suit in the circuit court for their freedom, the expenses being defrayed by a group of persons headed by Francis Scott Key, who gave his legal services gratis.

there are at present about 600 of them of both sexes and of every age from babe to old man or woman of 70. They are quartered in the two north houses of the row, the other houses being occupied by the military. The sexes are being kept separate except in the case of families, when they are assigned separate rooms from the others.

The houses, which sat where the Library of Congress now stands, were no better than the prison, according to African-American abolitionist writer Harriet Jacobs's report "Life among the Contrabands" in *The Liberator* in September 1862:

My first business would be to look into a small room on the ground floor. This room was covered with lime. Here I would learn how many deaths had occurred in the last twenty-four hours. Men, women and children lie here together, without a shadow of those rites which we give to our poorest dead. There they lie, in the filthy rags they wore from the plantation.

Nobody seems to give it a thought. It is an every-day occurrence, and the scenes have become familiar. One morning, as I looked in, I saw lying there five children. By the side of them lay a young man. He escaped, was taken back to Virginia, whipped nearly to death, escaped again the next night, dragged his body to Washington, and died, literally cut to pieces. Around his feet I saw a rope; I could not see that put into the grave with him. Other cases similar to this came to my knowledge, but this I saw.

Today there is nothing left of the Old Capitol Prison or Duff Green's Row. The two have been replaced by the Supreme Court building and the Library of Congress. The only acknowledgment of their existence is in books and a single plaque noting the former Old Capitol sitting near the Supreme Court building; the plaque does not mention the prison or any of the area's African-American history.

Lincoln Park (Statues of Abraham Lincoln and Mary McLeod Bethune)

Lincoln Park, located on East Capitol Street between Eleventh and Thirteenth Streets, is often frequented by baby-toting parents and frolicking dogs. But the park is historically significant for African Americans because of the two statues that sit in the middle: the Freedom's Memorial (also known as the Emancipation Statue) and a Mary McLeod Bethune statue called *Let Her Works Praise Her.*

The park itself was the first site to be named in honor of Abraham Lincoln after his assassination, with Congress authorizing it to be called Lincoln Square in 1867. It was a natural fit, the park having hosted Union troops and a medical center called Lincoln Hospital during the Civil War.

Freedom's Memorial: A Lincoln Statue, Paid for by Freed Slaves. The Freedom's Memorial was one of the first statues to honor Lincoln after his assassination by John Wilkes Booth, and one of the things that makes this statue unique is that it was almost entirely paid for by former slaves.

After the president's death, a freed Virginia slave named Charlotte Scott approached her employer in Marietta, Ohio, with the idea that African Americans should fund a statue to memorialize Lincoln in Washington, D.C. To back her idea, Scott donated the first $5 to the statue fund using the very first money she earned as a free woman.

The Freedom's Memorial

Following Scott's lead, many black military veterans and organizations in the African-American community started sending money to the memorial fund until finally the fund had enough money to support a bronze statue with a granite base. (One report suggests that the African-American community provided more than $16,000 of the $17,000 price tag of the statue.)

Once the money had been raised, managers of the memorial fund, called the Western Sanitary Commission, commissioned Thomas Ball, an American living in Italy, to create something worthy of Lincoln and the people who had donated their hard-earned money to honor his memory. Ball crafted a statue depicting Lincoln with the Emancipation Proclamation in his right hand and with his left extended over a kneeling slave, rising from the earth, shackles broken. Next to Lincoln is a monolith containing a bust of George Washington in relief. Around the monument's base is the word Emancipation, and on the front is the following inscription:

> Freedom's Memorial: In grateful memory of ABRAHAM LINCOLN, this monument was erected by the Western Sanitary Commission of St. Louis, MO with funds contributed solely by emancipated citizens of the United States, declared free by his proclamation, January 1, A.D., 1863. The first contribution of five dollars was made by Charlotte Scott, a freed woman of Virginia, being her first earnings in freedom, and consecrated by her suggestion and request, on the day she heard of President Lincoln's death, to build a monument to his memory.

Part of the Emancipation Proclamation appears on the back of the statue: "And upon this act, sincerely believed to be an act of justice, warranted by the Constitution upon military necessity, I invoke the considerate judgment of mankind and the gracious favor of Almighty God." Congress paid the remaining money needed to finish the statue, appropriating $3,000 for its ten-foot-high pedestal just in time for its unveiling on the eleventh anniversary of Lincoln's death on April 14, 1876.

In addition to being one of the first statues of Lincoln, the Freedom's Memorial also was the first statue of a black erected in the nation's capital. The kneeling slave in Freedom's Memorial is a model of an actual man named Archer Alexander who had been a slave in Missouri at the outbreak of the Civil War. According to his biography, *The Story of Archer Alexander: From Slavery to Freedom, March 30, 1863,* Alexander got himself in trouble for helping out some

Union soldiers. The author, William G. Eliot, said Alexander discovered that some Confederate sympathizers had sabotaged a bridge that would soon be used by Union troops: "At night he walked five miles to the house of a well-known Union man, through whom the intelligence and warning were conveyed to the Union troops, who repaired the bridge before crossing it," Eliot wrote. That move got Alexander in trouble with his master, and he had to flee the farm. But he was soon caught in Eliot's home, where he was being sheltered. Wrote Eliot:

> The three men had come in, with clubs in hand, and, getting close to where Archer was working, said, "Is your name Archie?"—"Yes, sir, I've no 'casion to deny my name."—"Well, let go that horse, you runaway rascal, and come with us."—"No, sir, I'se here under pertection of the law." He had no sooner said the word than one of them raised his bludgeon and knocked him down with a blow on the head. The others pulled out knives and pistols, and kicked him in the face. Then they handcuffed him and forcibly dragged the helpless man to their wagon, pushed him in, and drove off at the top of speed towards the city.

Alexander eventually escaped from the slave-catchers and returned to St. Louis, where he would live out the rest of his life. Eliot ended up on the commission deciding what kind of statue would go into Lincoln Park. The commission wanted a real escaped slave to model for the statue, and Eliot gave sculptor Thomas Ball a photograph of Alexander. Alexander was pleased when he found out that he would be forever connected with Lincoln through the statue in Washington. "When I showed to him the photographic picture of the 'Freedom's Memorial' monument, soon after its inauguration in Washington, and explained to him its meaning, and that he would thus be remembered in connection with Abraham Lincoln, the emancipator of his race, he laughed all over," Eliot wrote.

Statue of Mary McLeod Bethune. The second African American to be depicted in a statue in Washington, D.C., is educator Mary McLeod Bethune, who also holds the honor of being the first American woman and the only African-American woman to be depicted in a statue in the nation's capital. Bethune's statue was added to Lincoln Park on July 10, 1974, the ninety-ninth anniversary of her birth. The addition of the statue even affected the Freedom's Memorial, which pointed toward the Capitol until the Bethune statue was added to the park. Lincoln now faces Bethune, an appropriate position for these two great Americans.

Bethune was born on July 10, 1875, in Mayesville, South Carolina, to parents who were freed from slavery as a result of the Civil War. After her schooling was completed, she was determined that other opportunities be made available for African-American students. In 1904 she opened the Daytona Normal and Industrial Institute in Florida, where she served as president for nearly forty years. In 1923 the school merged with the Cookman Institute for men and was reborn as Bethune-Cookman College, a historically black institution in Daytona Beach, Florida.

Mary McLeod Bethune, founder of the National Council of Negro Women
LIBRARY OF CONGRESS, LC-USZ62-42476

Bethune was also active in politics, advocating for the rights of African Americans and women. She began the National Council of Negro Women in 1935 and was appointed by President Franklin D. Roosevelt as head of the Division of Negro Affairs of the National Youth Administration, the highest government position then held by a woman and the first time an African American headed a federal office.

The statue erected at the National Council of Negro Women is a modernist depiction of Bethune with a cane given to her by President Roosevelt in one hand and what looks like a scroll or a diploma, ready to be handed to a young black girl and boy, in the other hand.

Mary Jane McLeod Bethune died on May 18, 1955, and in addition to her statue in Lincoln Park, she was honored with a postage stamp in her name in 1985.

Southeast

Southeast Washington, D.C., is thought of as the "black" part of D.C. since it is home to the historically African-American neighborhood of Anacostia. The construction of the new Washington Nationals baseball stadium on the Anacostia River is leading a renaissance in this part of Washington, and there are several attractions worth seeing in this quadrant.

Anacostia Museum and Center for African American History and Culture, Smithsonian Museum

The Smithsonian Institution's Anacostia Museum and Center for African American History and Culture holds the unique position of being not only the first federally funded neighborhood museum in the United States, but also one of the most significant African-American-themed museums in the country. It was originally called the Anacostia Community Museum and the Anacostia

A Modest Community Museum

The idea for the Anacostia Neighborhood Museum developed in 1966, when Smithsonian secretary S. Dillon Ripley agreed to support the idea of a neighborhood museum and community outreach program.

After a discussion with community leaders in Anacostia, a primarily African-American neighborhood in southeast D.C., the Smithsonian purchased the Carver Theater in Anacostia as the site for the project in March 1967. The Carver Theater was renamed the Anacostia Neighborhood Museum, and it opened to the public on September 15, 1967, with six exhibits covering everything from community-related interests to national interests. Exhibits included a Mercury space capsule; a reproduction of an 1890 Anacostia store; a little theater; shoebox collections of many natural-science subjects; skeletons that could be disassembled; and a small zoo.

As the Anacostia Neighborhood Museum's collection grew, so did its need for more space and more funding. The museum had subsisted on special grants, but in 1970 it finally became a line item in the Smithsonian Institution's federal budget, making it the first federally funded community museum.

The space issue was resolved in 1974, when the exhibit branch of the museum was moved to an Exhibits Design and Production Laboratory in Fort Stanton Park. That facility would become the foundation for the current museum building, which was finished in 1987. In April of that year, the Anacostia Neighborhood Museum became the Smithsonian Institution Anacostia Community Museum.

Neighborhood Museum; the name change to Anacostia Museum and Center for African American History and Culture illustrates the growth of this museum from "an experimental store-front museum" to a major custodian of African-American history in Washington, D.C.

The museum's collection today includes more than six thousand artifacts and features significant holdings in art, religion, photography, and family history dating to the early 1800s. Some of the significant pieces in the museum's collection include the 1802 edition of Phillis Wheatley's book *Poems on Various Subjects, Religious and Moral,* the first book published in the United States by an African American. Also in the archives are works from Dudley Randall's Broadside Press and Carter G. Woodson's Associated Publishers, as well as artwork from such nationally known artists as Elena Bland, John Robinson, Lou Stovall, James Wells, Radcliffe Bailey, and Leslie Payne.

The Anacostia Museum and Center for African American History and Culture has not forgotten its neighborhood roots. The museum also features rotating exhibits dealing with Washington, D.C., and African-American communities.

Frederick Douglass National Historic Site

The Frederick Douglass National Historic Site is the location of Douglass's final home in the District of Columbia—Cedar Hill, which Douglass bought in 1877. To this day the immaculate home and spacious estate grounds are kept in much the same way as they were during Douglass's seventeen years there. The rooms are filled with items from his personal life, including books, letters, and even gifts from his friends (including President Abraham Lincoln). Paintings of the people he knew and the places he visited still hang on the walls, a checkerboard sits ready for another game, and his violin is ready for another tune. On his desk in the library, a pair of glasses and a pen sit waiting for Douglass to write another one of his stirring speeches. Douglass wrote his last autobiography in this library (*The Life and Times of Frederick Douglass,* 1892), which is where the famous photograph of him working at his desk was taken.

On the wall of the front hall at Cedar Hill is a dramatic painting of the 54th Massachusetts Volunteer Infantry Regiment storming Fort Wagner in South Carolina. Most people know this scene and the 54th Massachusetts from the movie *Glory.* Douglass had a dual interest in the 54th Massachusetts: He served

Frederick Douglass
LIBRARY OF CONGRESS, LC-BH832-30219

as a major recruiter for the volunteer unit and he was one of the major advocates to President Lincoln for adding African Americans to the Union Army. He also had a personal interest in the 54th Massachusetts because his two sons, Lewis and Charles Douglass, served as volunteers in the unit. Lewis ended up being promoted to sergeant major, the highest rank available to black soldiers at that time. He was wounded at Fort Wagner but survived.

One of the interesting facts about Cedar Hill is that there are two bedrooms in the house for Douglass's two wives. Douglass's original wife and the mother of his children, Anna Murray, died in 1882 after he moved into Cedar Hill. The next year, Douglass shocked American society by marrying a white woman who was nearly twenty years his junior, his former secretary, Helen Pitts, of Rochester, New York. Pitts was a graduate of Mount Holyoke Seminary and daughter of Gideon Pitts Jr., an abolitionist colleague and friend of Douglass. She was also a cousin to Presidents John Adams and John Quincy Adams.

Douglass thought nothing of the controversy. He said that with his first wife he had honored his mother's race, and with his second wife he was honoring his father's. (This was not Douglass's first relationship with a white woman. He had carried on a long affair with Ottilie Assing, a German journalist who in 1857 spent the first of twenty-two summers living in the Douglass family home. After Douglass married Pitts, Assing learned that she had cancer and committed suicide—but not before naming Frederick Douglass as the sole heir in her will.)

During the years Douglass lived at Cedar Hill, he devoted himself to African-American and women's rights. After returning to America from Haiti in 1891, he threw himself back into his writing and his work with the antilynching movement and women's suffrage. Douglass attended the first Women's Rights convention at Seneca Falls, New York, in 1848 with feminist Elizabeth Cady Stanton. He spoke in favor of women's suffrage, frequently proclaiming, "rights know no race or sex." In fact, Douglass had attended a meeting of the National Council of Women in Washington, D.C., on February 20, 1895, the day he died. During that meeting, he was brought to the platform and given a standing ovation by the audience. He died of heart failure shortly after he returned home to Cedar Hill.

Douglass's family held a private family funeral for their patriarch at Cedar Hill before allowing his body to lie in state at Metropolitan African Methodist Church in Washington. Douglass was buried in Rochester, New York.

After Frederick Douglass's death, his wife Helen bequeathed Cedar Hill to the congressionally chartered Frederick Douglass Memorial and Historical Association. The association, along with the National Association of Colored Women's Clubs, opened the house to visitors in 1916. Added to the national park system in 1962, Cedar Hill became the Frederick Douglass National Historic Site when it was designated a national historic site in 1988.

Northwest

The Northwest quadrant of Washington, D.C., holds most of the city's official monuments and attractions. But that doesn't mean that there aren't also hidden gems worth seeing in this part of the District of Columbia.

Mary McLeod Bethune Council House National Historic Site

Mary McLeod Bethune is one of America's most honored women, having earned both a public statue in Washington, D.C., and national-historic-site status for her house in the nation's capital.

The Mary McLeod Bethune Council House National Historic Site was purchased by Mary McLeod Bethune and her organization, the National Council of

Negro Women (NCNW), in 1943 for $15,500. The Victorian town house on 1318 Vermont Avenue NW, known as the Council House, served as the National Council of Negro Women's headquarters and Bethune's personal residence until 1949. From the Council House, the NCNW entertained people such as First Lady Eleanor Roosevelt and planned such crusades as the integration of African Americans into the military and the public education system. From this location they also worked toward solving problems like racial discrimination and inadequate housing, health care, and employment.

In 1975 the Council House was declared a historic site by the District of Columbia, which placed it on the Washington, D.C., Register of Historic Sites, and restoration began. In November 1979 the Council House reopened to the public as a museum and archive of African-American women's history. In 1982 Congress declared the Council House a National Historic Site, and the National Park Service purchased the property and renamed it the Mary McLeod Bethune Council House National Historic Site in 1994.

National Archives for Black Women's History. The National Archives for Black Women's History at the Bethune Council House is the only archive devoted to African-American women's history in the United States. The archives include material about Mary McLeod Bethune, the National Council of Negro Women, other African-American women's organizations, and individuals associated with those organizations, focusing on the years of Mary McLeod Bethune's life, 1875–1955. *Mary McLeod Bethune Council House National Historic Site; 1318 Vermont Avenue NW, Washington, D.C.; 202-673-2402.*

African American Civil War Memorial and Museum

The African American Civil War Memorial. The African American Civil War Memorial is the only monument to black soldiers in the majority-black District of Columbia, honoring all of the colored troops who served in the Civil War. It is also the first memorial in the entire nation to honor black Civil War soldiers.

Located on U Street, known as "Black Broadway" because of its strong African-American business life and culture (and because of famous residents like Duke Ellington), the majestic African American Civil War Memorial was dedicated on July 18, 1998. The centerpiece statue, the *Spirit of Freedom* by Ed

Hamilton, was the first major art piece created by a black sculptor to be placed on federal land anywhere in the nation's capital.

A ten-foot bronze piece sitting on a two-foot-high round base, the *Spirit of Freedom* features three uniformed African-American soldiers and a sailor poised to leave home and fight for their freedom and their country. On the back, the monument depicts in relief a family surrounding a soldier—their son—as he leaves for the war. Women, children, and elders on the cusp of the concave inner surface seek strength together.

Surrounding the *Spirit of Freedom* on three sides is a Wall of Honor where the names of 209,145 United States Colored Troops who served in the Civil War are listed according to regiment on 157 burnished stainless-steel plaques, including the names of the 7,000 white officers who served with the African-American troops. (Appropriately, the part of the District of Columbia where the memorial sits is called the Shaw neighborhood. It was named after Col. Robert Gould Shaw, the leader of the famed 54th Massachusetts Volunteer Infantry Regiment. A fictional-ized version of their story was told in the hit movie *Glory.*)

The African American Civil War Memorial Museum. Only a few steps away from the African American Civil War Memorial is the museum. The major portion of this collection documents the participation of African Americans in the Civil War, including printed and handwritten orders, posters, military sou-

Ed Hamilton

Sculptor Ed Hamilton of Louisville, Kentucky, also designed the statue of Booker T. Washington in the Booker T. Washington Memorial Garden at

Hampton University in Hampton, Virginia; the Amistad Memorial in New Haven, Connecticut; and the Joe Louis Memorial inside the Cobo Center in Detroit, Michigan. Hamilton also recently completed a statue of York, the slave of William Clark, for Louisville, Ken-tucky. (York was a vital part of the Lewis and Clark Expedition of 1803–1806.) He also has published his autobiography, *The Birth of an Artist: A Journey of Discovery.*

The African American Civil War Memorial

venirs, and images of soldiers and their families. The museum also has stored the
letters written by soldiers detailing camp life and the battles in which they
fought so courageously.

Located two blocks west of the memorial, the museum opened in 1999 and
features displays like "Slavery to Freedom," which documents the largely unher-
alded struggle of slaves and freedmen during Civil War times using photographs,
documents, and state-of-the-art audiovisual equipment. Museum workers also
are trained to help visitors find information about relatives who may have fought
with the United States Colored Troops or helped the Union in other ways.

African-American men were employed as carpenters, cooks, laborers, teamsters, and surgeons. They also worked in infantry and artillery companies. Black men and some women, such as Harriet Tubman, served as nurses, scouts, and even spies. However they served, African-American men and women were crucial to the Union Army.

By the end of the Civil War, the United States Colored Troops had formed 166 regiments, and one in twelve soldiers who served in the Union Army was African American. About ten thousand African-American soldiers died in battle, and three times as many died from illness. African-American sailors also acquitted themselves admirably and served honorably. By the end of the war, fourteen African-American soldiers and eight sailors had won the Congressional Medal of Honor.

Theodore Roosevelt Island National Memorial (Analostan Island)

Theodore Roosevelt Island National Memorial is one of those often-overlooked monuments in Washington, D.C., because it sits in the middle of the Potomac River instead of on the National Mall.

Accessible only from the George Washington Parkway in Virginia, the ninety-one-acre wooded island is a monument to the twenty-sixth president, who was best known as an outstanding naturalist and outdoorsman. During his time in the White House, Roosevelt preserved more than 234 million acres of national parks, forests, monuments, and wildlife refuges, and he established the U.S. Forest Service.

Roosevelt also was an impressive president. He was an early supporter of civil and women's rights, and he was the head honcho behind the construction of the Panama Canal. In addition, Roosevelt was the first American to win the Nobel Peace Prize, which he received for negotiating the end of the Russo-Japanese War. He was also the first president to use the phrase "White House" as an official title instead of a nickname.

The Teddy Bear and Holt Collier. Theodore Roosevelt might be most famous for his association with a toy—the teddy bear. This legacy is directly related to circumstances involving an African American.

Roosevelt, an avid hunter, went down to Mississippi to hunt black bears in

1902. Since Roosevelt was the president and a failed bear hunt would be an embarrassment, the organizers partnered Roosevelt with an African-American hunter named Holt Collier. Collier, a former slave and Confederate soldier, had become known as the best bear hunter in the United States, bagging more than three thousand bears in his lifetime. His reputation was so great that he was asked to go with Roosevelt on the famous bear hunt.

While the popular story is that Roosevelt refused to shoot the defenseless bear on his own, Collier told an interviewer: "It was going to be a ten day hunt, but the President was impatient. 'I must see a live bear the first day,' he said. I told him he would if I had to tie one and bring it to him. Mr. Foote made fun of me. The President looked doubtful, but Mr. Percy and Major Helm said I could do it." Collier then tracked down an old bear to a lake, wrestled him out of the water, and tied him to a tree.

> I went to camp and brought 'em down to see the bear. I had tied it but wouldn't take it to the President like I'd said I would. When they all got there the President ran into the water, and I said to him, with my head down, 'Don't shoot him while he's tied.' Everybody tried to get him to do it but he couldn't," Collier said. ". . . Back in camp that night the President told me I was the best guide and hunter he'd ever seen. Mr. Foote didn't laugh at that either.

Roosevelt's mercy for the bear that Collier caught for him ended up being portrayed in a nationwide newspaper cartoon. Seeing that cartoon, a toymaker came up with a great idea for a new toy for children—a teddy bear.

Civil War Training Ground for the First District Colored Volunteer Regiment. After Roosevelt's death on January 6, 1919, the Theodore Roosevelt Memorial Association purchased the Potomac River island in 1932 as a permanent tribute to the conservationist president. Congress approved funds for a memorial in 1960, and Eric Gugler designed the formal memorial to be placed in the northern center of the island. Inside the memorial is a seventeen-foot bronze statue of Roosevelt, designed and created by Paul Manship. The statue stands in front of a thirty-foot-high shaft of granite that overlooks an oval terrace. The surrounding terrace features four twenty-one-foot granite tablets inscribed with the tenets of Roosevelt's philosophy of citizenship.

The island had a history before being named after Theodore Roosevelt, however. The Indians called it "Analostan" and used it for fishing. But more importantly, Analostan Island was also the Civil War training ground for the First District Colored Volunteer Regiment, the first black regiment to be formally mustered into federal service during the Civil War.

The First Regiment was the brainchild of two white chaplains, J. D. Turner and W. G. Raymond, and it was led by Rev. Henry McNeal Turner, the famed leader of the Israel Bethel African Methodist Episcopal Church. President Lincoln agreed to the formation of the First Regiment after signing the Emancipation Proclamation in January 1863, and Turner and Raymond began posting notices and recruiting for the first "Colored Regiment in the District of Columbia."

The First Regiment faced the same racism and distrust that black troops would face for decades to come. On this front, the District of Columbia was not much different from other southern cities, with its own "Black Codes," slave pens, and organized racism. Harassment of individual black soldiers was commonplace in Washington, D.C. Out of fear that white Washingtonians would become violent if they saw a regiment of uniformed black soldiers in their city, the black recruits were sent to train on Analostan Island on the Potomac River just south of Georgetown. Government officials were so worried about the reaction of white Washingtonians to uniformed blacks that it is said that not even President Lincoln knew the location of their camp.

Poet Walt Whitman, who served as a volunteer in Union Army hospitals, is said to have praised the First Regiment. "There are getting to be many black troops. There is one very good regt. here black as tar; they go around, have the regular uniform—they submit to no nonsense. Others are constantly forming. It is getting to be a common sight," Whitman wrote in June 1863.

On Analostan Island the recruits rose with the sun and spent the day doing military drills. Once they were ready, they headed to Camp Greene in North Carolina, where they eventually joined Brig. Gen. Edward A. Wild's "African Brigade." When they shipped out, the First District Colored Volunteer Regiment consisted of more than 1,200 officers and men from all over the eastern seaboard states, Canada, and the Caribbean, with at least one-third coming from Virginia. Led by white officers, the First Regiment would go on to distinguish itself in combat in North Carolina and Virginia at battles like Chaffin's Farm, Fair Oaks, and Fort Fisher.

They also participated in the battle of Wilson's Wharf, which was likely the only battle in the Civil War that was fought by all-black Union troops. Gen. Fitzhugh Lee, the nephew of Robert E. Lee, led about three thousand men in an attack on the Union supply depot at Wilson's Wharf, which sits on the James River in eastern Charles City, Virginia. Lee's troops were defeated by about 1,800 members of the United States Colored Troops, including the First Regiment, under the command of Brig. Gen. Edward Wild.

By the end of the Civil War, the men of the First Regiment were so esteemed that when they were mustered out on September 29, 1865, they were invited to return to the District to meet the president. This marked the first time African-American military men were formally received by the President of the United States at the White House. President Andrew Johnson was so impressed with the men of the First Regiment that he advocated voting rights for veterans of the United States Colored Troops.

The men of the First Regiment have no memorial on their training ground on Analostan Island, but their names are inscribed on the African American Civil War Memorial in downtown Washington, D.C. This is the only memorial to the first African-American regiment to be formally mustered into federal service.

Stephen Decatur House and Slave Quarters

The Stephen Decatur House in Lafayette Square holds a unique place in the District of Columbia's history, as this 1818 home was both the first and the last private residence built and occupied on Lafayette Square near the White House. The name of the house comes from the famed naval hero, Com. Stephen Decatur, who lived in the house with his wife Susan. It is one of only three remaining residential buildings in the country designed by Benjamin Henry Latrobe, the father of American architecture, who was responsible for many of the city's earliest buildings, including St. John's Church, the Washington Navy Yard, and portions of the White House and the U.S. Capitol.

More important, the Decatur House is one of the few buildings in the District of Columbia that still has its slave quarters intact and available for public viewing. The portion of the house built as the living quarters for slaves is not original, having been added in 1839 after the Decatur House came into the possession of John Gadsby, an Alexandria, Virginia, businessman, hotelier, and

John Gadsby's Will

When John Gadsby died on May 15, 1844, he left all of his possessions to his wife Provey, including the Decatur House and the slaves that lived there:

> To wife, all the following negro slaves: man Nace, or Ignatius Newton, aged about 50 yrs.; man Henry King, aged about 40 yrs.; woman Maria King, aged about 35 yrs.; girl Celia King, aged about 16 yrs.; boy Charles King, aged about 9 yrs.; girl Sarah Jane King, aged about 4 yrs.; boy George King, aged about 18 mos.; woman Maria Williams, aged about 30 yrs.; girl Martha Ann Williams, aged about 6 yrs.; girl Mary Ellen Williams, aged about 4 yrs.; boy James Williams, aged about 18 mos.; woman Keziah Williams, aged about 28 yrs.; Mary Frances Williams, aged about 7 yrs.; boy William Williams, aged about 5 yrs.; woman Rosa Marks, aged about 48 yrs.; Nancy Fairfax, aged about 45 yrs.; James Long, aged about 25 yrs. Also to wife, all household furniture, plate, pictures, library, groceries, liquors, linen, garden and other implements and utensils, horses and carriage, hay, grain, harness.

slave trader. Susan Decatur, the wife of Stephen Decatur, was forced to sell the Decatur House in 1836 after her husband was killed in a duel. Gadsby bought the elegant house and continued to entertain Washington society from his exclusive location in Lafayette Square, although his profession was frowned upon by some of the dignitaries who came to call. According to the book *Historic Houses of George-Town & Washington City,* Gadsby was described by one of his guests like this: "He is an old wretch who has made a fortune in the slave trade, which does not prevent Washington society from rushing to his house, and I should make my government very unpopular if I refused to associate with this kind of people."

When Gadsby bought the Decatur House, there wasn't enough room for all of his slaves, so he made a major addition to the house: a two-story service wing where his slaves could live and work. Years later, the house was turned into a museum and the service wing was turned into office space, but the slaves who lived in the Decatur House went unacknowledged. The service wing, which runs along the H Street side of the house, now serves as the exhibit gallery and gift shop. Inside the exhibit gallery visitors can see the original fireplace that existed in the slave quarters. The gallery also contains handwritten documents that out-line some of the slaves who lived in this house.

A Tribute to Charlotte Dupuy. Only one of the slaves who lived in the Decatur House is memorialized with an exhibit inside the museum. That slave is Charlotte Dupuy, a Kentucky-born slave who actually sued her master—the famed orator, politician, and presidential candidate Henry Clay—for her freedom.

Clay owned Dupuy, her husband Aaron, and their two children, and he moved them to the Decatur House in 1827. (At that time the Decaturs were renting out the house.) When Clay's term in the House of Representatives ended in 1829, Lotty Dupuy acted quickly. Clay was ready to move Dupuy and her family back to Kentucky, where her life as a slave would be fixed forever. Instead of going quietly, Lotty Dupuy filed suit with the U.S. Circuit Court for the District of Columbia, petitioning for freedom for herself and her two children.

Dupuy's claim was that her previous owner, the man who sold her and her family to Clay, had promised to release them after a certain amount of time. Filing the suit was a small victory in itself because, pending the outcome of the case, Clay was ordered by the court to leave Dupuy behind in Washington when he left for Kentucky. She continued to live in the Decatur House and was employed by the house's next occupant, then Secretary of State and future U.S. president Martin Van Buren.

Unfortunately for Dupuy, she eventually lost her case to Clay. The court ruled that any agreement between Dupuy and her previous owner could not be applied to Clay, and therefore she was still his property. After winning the court case, Clay asked Dupuy to return to Kentucky voluntarily, but she refused. Eventually, she was forcibly returned to Clay's possession in Kentucky. Dupuy would eventually gain her freedom, however. She became a free woman on October 12, 1840, while living in New Orleans with Henry Clay's daughter.

Charlotte Dupuy's dramatic story has now been woven into the interpretation of a room recently discovered to have been a kitchen, an area where she almost certainly would have spent much of her time inside the Decatur House.

Patrick Francis Healy Hall at Georgetown University

Georgetown University is considered to be one of the finest educational institutions in the world and is both the oldest Roman Catholic and the oldest Jesuit university in the United States. Located in the Georgetown neighborhood of the District of Columbia, the university also holds a significant place in American history for being the first major university to appoint an African American as its president. That president was Rev. Patrick Francis Healy, who served as the twenty-ninth president of Georgetown University from 1874 to 1882. Healy is often referred to as the university's "second founder."

Healy was born in Georgia in 1834 to a slave mother of mixed blood and an Irish father. Since Healy's parents looked more Irish than African, Healy's father sent him and his brothers up north to ensure that they would be educated and free. (In Georgia the children of slaves were also considered to be slaves, a fate that the elder Healy wanted to spare his children.)

Educated by Quakers in New York State, Healy received a bachelor's degree from Holy Cross College in 1850 and joined the Jesuit order. He was the first African American to become a Jesuit priest. After graduating from Holy Cross, Healy left for Europe to continue his education. Once there, he earned his doctorate from the University of Louvain in Belgium in 1865, becoming the first American of openly acknowledged part-African descent to do so.

A year later, Healy arrived at Georgetown University to take a position on staff as a philosophy teacher. By 1873 Healy had risen through the ranks to become president of the university. When Healy took over, Georgetown University was still a sometimes-struggling college trying to find its way in the post–Civil War era. Healy is credited with turning the sleepy little university into the Georgetown University that we recognize today.

Under his leadership the university began a campus-wide beautification program, added sciences to the curriculum, organized an alumni outreach program, and revamped the medical and law schools. But the greatest project of Healy's tenure would be the one that he is remembered for now: Healy Hall.

Healy wanted a building that would make Georgetown stand out in the District of Columbia and that would provide the university with space for laboratories and a new library, as well as classrooms, dormitory rooms, and a meeting space for alumni. Healy went to the architects that designed the Library of Congress and requested a building of Romanesque architectural design with a 209-foot tower patterned after buildings he had seen during his time in Europe.

Getting the $300,000 needed for the building was a constant struggle for the Georgetown president, whose empty university coffers forced him to solicit donations from Georgetown's neighbors in Washington, D.C. To make matters worse, rumors about Healy's parentage began to spread in the District of Columbia just as the building was half complete. All of the sudden, locals in the nation's capital refused to donate any more money to Georgetown.

Healy then turned to an untapped resource—Georgetown alumni. He spent years traveling around the country soliciting donations from former Georgetown students. Finally, two years after ground was broken on the building, Healy Hall was complete. It was the first building on Georgetown's campus that faced the District of Columbia instead of the Potomac River.

Healy spent most of his time traveling the country and raising money to help pay off the debt for Healy Hall, and the constant travel took its toll on his health. He died in 1910, and his body was brought back to Georgetown to be buried in the Jesuit cemetery.

It turns out that Healy's $300,000 investment in a new building for Georgetown University paid off. The current replacement value for Healy Hall, which was placed on the National Register of Historic Places in 1988, is now estimated to be more than $30 million. But the emotional value of the building that has come to symbolize one of the finest universities in the world and its groundbreaking president is incalculable.

DISCOVERING BLACK HISTORY IN MARYLAND

Any examination of African-American history in the nation's capital would be sorely lacking without the inclusion of the District's two closest neighbors, Maryland and Virginia. Washington, D.C., is forever tied to those two states: Land for the District was given to the federal government by the states of Virginia and Maryland for the city's founding in 1790. Even today, very few people come to Washington, D.C., without setting foot in the District's northern and southern neighbors.

Most people consider Virginia the birthplace of African-American history, with John Rolfe's Jamestown journal of August 20, 1619, recording that "there came in a Dutch man-of-warre that sold us 20 negars." While this was not the first appearance of Africans in North America (Spaniards brought Africans to the Americas as slaves in 1526), Virginia unquestionably has played a tremendous role in the history of African Americans in this country. The same goes for Maryland, the birthplace of such famous African Americans as abolitionist Frederick Douglass; freedom fighter Harriet Tubman; Josiah Henson, of *Uncle Tom's Cabin* fame; Arctic explorer Matthew Henson; scientist Benjamin Banneker; and others.

A true examination of Virginia and Maryland's African-American history and landmarks requires more space than is available here. However, there are some places within reach of the District of Columbia that should appeal to anyone interested in African-American history.

Montgomery County

Montgomery County, one of the affluent and influential counties in Maryland, has a strong African-American history and attractions you'll miss if you don't explore outside the District.

Sandy Spring Slave Museum and African Art Gallery, Sandy Spring

Slavery got its start in America in the Mid-Atlantic States, with thousands of slaves being brought across the Atlantic Ocean on slave ships into the United States. The Sandy Spring Slavery Museum and African Art Gallery is one of the few places modern Americans can get a taste of the horrid, cramped conditions slaves suffered on the long trip across the sea. Open by appointment only, the museum features a freestanding, life-size cross-section of a slave clipper ship that people can enter to see the conditions the slaves on these vessels faced. Also on hand is a real slavery-era log cabin from nearby Olney, Maryland, that shows the conditions slaves lived in once they made it to America.

The Sandy Spring Slave Museum and African Art Gallery also features an arts pavilion in the design of an African hut, where tourists can see textiles, instruments, and furniture from the continent of Africa. The newest addition to the museum is a Great Hall, which houses local slavery and civil rights documents, including manumission papers, more African art, and other artifacts (such as an array of shackles and an authentic Ku Klux Klan costume). *Sandy Spring Slave Museum & African Art Gallery; 18524 Brooke Road, Sandy Spring, MD; 301-384-0727.*

Oakley Cabin, Brookville

The Oakley Cabin is an outstanding example of how the "other half" lived during slavery and Jim Crow times in the South's antebellum days. Built around 1800, the Oakley Cabin was likely the slave quarters for the Oakley/Dorsey farm before becoming living quarters for freed black families following the Civil War. The mansion that belonged to that farm is long gone, but this rustic dwelling with its hand-hewn logs of oak and chestnut still stands and now operates as a living-history site and museum.

Billing itself as the only publicly owned African-American historical site in

Lincoln Credited Harriet Beecher Stowe with Starting the Civil War

Harriet Beecher Stowe's novel *Uncle Tom's Cabin* is credited with fanning the flames of the Civil War with its depiction of the horrible conditions that slaves lived under in the antebellum South. Stowe's

description of a ragged old slave being repeatedly beaten was so powerful and instrumental in the anti-slavery movement in the North that, upon meeting her, President Abraham Lincoln is said to have commented: "So this is the little lady who started this big war!"

Montgomery County open to the public, Oakley Cabin is furnished to depict the various periods of its history and development. Once inside the multistory cabin, one can begin to learn more about how African Americans built a world of their own even in the most trying situations.

On the ground floor of the cabin are exhibits using authentic period and replica collection pieces to show how families lived, worked, and survived together. The exhibits also display nineteenth-century tools used to construct cabins like this one, as well as excavated artifacts from the people who lived in this dwelling.

Upstairs is the private world of the African-American family, where as many as ten members of the family slept (slaves slept on a corn husk mattress, while the more affluent sharecropper or freedman farmer was upgraded to an iron frame bed) and kept all their valuables and food for the winter. The cabin is open the last Saturday of every month from noon to 4:00 p.m. *Oakley Cabin; 3610 Brookeville Road, Brookeville, MD; 301-563-3405.*

Uncle Tom's Cabin, Bethesda

Although *Uncle Tom's Cabin* is a novel, it is based on a real person and a real place that is now open to the public in Bethesda, Maryland, minutes outside of Washington, D.C. Josiah Henson, an escaped slave from Montgomery County,

The Underground Railroad, *a painting by Chas. T. Webber*

Maryland, and his 1849 autobiography, *The Life of Josiah Henson, Formerly a Slave,* are believed to have been the inspiration for Harriet Beecher Stowe's novel *Uncle Tom's Cabin.* The cabin where Henson and other slaves lived—the real "Uncle Tom's Cabin"—still stands in Bethesda. The state of Maryland bought the property in January 2006 and plans to turn it into either a house museum or a center for African-American studies.

Nestled in between several modern million-dollar homes, the thirteen-by-seventeen-foot cabin stands out with its gray stone chimney, antique wooden door, and solitary white-paned window. While the cabin now has hardwood floors, Henson described it in his book as having a dirt floor. He also described slaves' living quarters in the cabin:

> Our lodging was in log huts, of a single small room, with no other floor than the trodden earth, in which ten or a dozen persons—men, women, and children—might sleep, but which could not protect them from dampness and cold, nor permit the existence of the common decencies of life. There were neither beds, nor furniture of any description—a blanket being the only addition to the dress of the day for protection from the chillness of the

air or the earth. In these hovels were we penned at night, and fed by day; here were the children born, and the sick—neglected. Such were the provisions for the daily toil of the slave.

Although he is most commonly recognized as the inspiration for the character of Uncle Tom, Henson himself is also worth remembering. After escaping to Canada, he wrote his autobiography (a later edition of his autobiography, called *Truth Is Stranger Than Fiction,* contains a preface written by Harriet Beecher Stowe), toured Canada and England as a Methodist minister and speaker for abolitionist causes, founded a settlement and school for other escaped slaves in Canada, and served as a conductor on the famed Underground Railroad, ushering other slaves to freedom. He also became the first black person to be honored on a Canadian postage stamp. *Uncle Tom's Cabin; 11420 Old Georgetown Road, Bethesda, MD.*

Matthew Henson, First Man at the North Pole. Josiah Henson's greatgrandnephew, Matthew Henson, is honored as being the first man to stand on the North Pole. He accompanied Adm. Robert Peary on his expedition to the North Pole, and he beat Peary to the spot in 1909. There is a plaque to Matthew Henson inside the state capitol in Annapolis, Maryland.

Prince George's County, Mitchellville

Prince George's County is the wealthiest majority African-American county in the nation, so it has several historical African-American sites to visit. (Tip: Don't call it "PG County." The residents *hate* that.)

Northampton Plantation Slave Quarters

For centuries, Northampton was a classic *Gone with the Wind*–style Southern plantation, complete with a "big house," tobacco fields, and slave shanties. Now, little is left of Northampton except a crumbling plantation house, decrepit outbuildings, and the slave quarters. The remnants of the slaves' living quarters, which sit near modern town houses and luxury homes, are now the focus of the Northampton Plantation Slave Quarters, an outdoor museum where visitors can explore how slaves lived on a plantation between the 1600s and 1800s and how they transitioned from slavery to tenant farming to the modern economy. Featuring the rebuilt foundations of the two slave quarters, the site also has signs

The Northampton Plantation Slave Quarters Archeological Site

depicting how enslaved and free African Americans lived on Northampton and what happened to their descendants after the plantation closed. One of the two slave quarters is of special interest to historians because it was made of brick instead of wood, which was unusual for slave quarters in the South. Each October the descendents of Elizabeth Savoy Hawkins, one of the slaves who lived at Northampton, return to celebrate the dedication of the site. Educational and interpretative programs also are available by appointment. *Northampton Plantation Slave Quarters Archeological Site; 100700 Lake Overlook Drive, Lake Arbor Community, Mitchellville, MD; 301-627-1286.*

Howard County, Columbia

Howard County Center of African American Culture

Just minutes outside the Washington Beltway sits one of Maryland's most impressive African-American collections: the Howard County Center of African American Culture.

Fans of both antique and modern African-American memorabilia will love this museum, which sits demurely in a small building next to the massive Oakland Mansion, a restored 1811 mansion that is one of the oldest buildings in

Howard County. The center boasts an extensive collection of African-American memorabilia dating as far back as the 1800s. The display pieces are laid out as they would have been in the home of a middle-class or wealthy African-American family of the time period. The layout includes boot jacks in the parlor, washboards, cast-iron skillets in the kitchen, and old-fashioned radio consoles in the living room.

Artifacts that are recognizable to older African Americans aren't all that's to be found in this museum. It also features an impressive compilation of items that younger African Americans will recognize, including collectibles like the first Wheaties box featuring an African-American athlete (Walter Payton) and the first cereal box featuring an African-American woman (Kellogg's Corn Flakes with Vanessa Williams); dolls representing Flip Wilson/Geraldine, M.C. Hammer, and Michael Jackson; a bag of Mohammad Ali potato chips; and an extensive collection of African-American records, stamps, books, and photographs, including a real photograph of the Wild West Buffalo soldiers. *Howard County Center of African-American Culture; 5434 Vantage Point Road, Columbia, MD; 410-715-1921.*

Howard County Center of African American Culture

African Art Museum of Maryland

African Art Museum of Maryland

Located inside the stately and historic Oakland Manor in Columbia, the African Art Museum of Maryland is a labor of love for its supporters. The brainchild of a former volunteer at the Smithsonian Institution National Museum of African Art in Washington, D.C., the museum boasts an impressive collection of African masks, sculptures, textiles, baskets, jewelry, household items, and musical instruments. It was founded in 1980 as the only museum in the nation established by African Americans for the display of African art. The museum and its founder, Doris Ligon, use its intimate two-room space to offer visitors an in-depth look at arts and crafts from Africa as a way to foster greater understanding of the continent's art.

Only a portion of the museum's 2,500-piece collection is on display at any given time. There is an extra gallery available on the first floor for disabled patrons since the main galleries are only accessible by stairs. In addition to its on-site exhibits, the museum also occasionally offers video presentations, lectures, films, youth and adult workshops, dance and music performances, visiting scholars, and lectures for its patrons. *African Art Museum of Maryland; 5430 Vantage Point Road, Columbia, MD; 410-730-4801.*

Minutes from the Maryland State Line

Harpers Ferry National Historical Park

Many people consider Harpers Ferry National Historical Park the place where the Civil War truly began. It was at this site in 1859 that abolitionist John Brown, considered by some to be the most controversial man of the nineteenth century, gathered his own army to begin a slave insurrection in the South. Brown's audacious plan may have failed, but his attempt electrified the nation and made him a martyr in the North. The place where Brown had his only victory (the takeover of a federal armory and arsenal from which he planned to arm slaves and take

over the state of Virginia) is now a national park covering more than 2,300 acres in the states of West Virginia, Maryland, and Virginia. The park, located at the confluence of the Potomac and Shenandoah Rivers, includes the town of Harpers Ferry, West Virginia, only minutes from the Maryland state line.

John Brown
LIBRARY OF CONGRESS,
LC-USZ62-2472

African Americans played a large part in the events that led to Brown's capture by federal forces, as well as in his trial for treason against the state of Virginia and his execution by hanging. One of the men John Brown wanted to have with him during his raid on Virginia was famed speaker and abolitionist Frederick Douglass. Brown's plan was to steal the guns at the federal armory, arm the hundreds of thousands of slaves who were being held in Virginia, and then sweep south, picking up more slaves along the way.

Douglass wanted nothing to do with the plan. He later wrote in his final autobiography *The Life and Times of Frederick Douglass,* "I at once opposed the measure with all the arguments at my command. To me such a measure would be fatal to running off slaves (as was the original plan), and fatal to all engaged in doing so. It would be an attack upon the Federal government, and would array the whole country against us."

It seemed at first that Douglass would be wrong. Brown's army of seventeen white and five black men easily captured the federal arsenal on October 16, 1859, from its sole watchman. They took hostages (including Col. Lewis Washington, great-grandnephew of George Washington), cut the telegraph lines, and waited for the expected legions of slaves to show up to join Brown's army. But things started falling apart quickly for the "Provisional Army of the United States." An unexpected train rolled into Harpers Ferry, and when the train's engineers refused to stop for Brown's men, the raiders opened fire. The only person killed by Brown's men was Hayward Shepherd, a free black man. Ironically, this free African-American man was the first victim of Brown's attempt to free other African Americans.

After Shepherd's death, Brown ordered that the train be allowed to continue on its way, and the news of the raid quickly reached Washington, D.C. Instead of attracting slaves who were desperate to be free, Brown's raid drew militia companies and federal troops from Maryland, Virginia, and the District of Columbia, including Marines commanded by Robert E. Lee and J.E.B. Stuart. They offered Brown a chance to surrender. Brown refused, and on October 18, 1859, they stormed the armory, leaving three locals, two of Brown's sons, and twelve others dead. Brown was beaten unconscious and dragged away for trial.

Brown, charged with "conspiring with slaves to commit treason and murder," was tried, convicted, and hanged in Charles Town, Virginia (now Charlestown, West Virginia), on December 2, 1859. (Two of the people who came to see Brown hanged were Thomas J. Jackson, later to be immortalized as "Stonewall" Jackson in the first Battle of Bull Run, and actor John Wilkes Booth, who would go on to assassinate President Abraham Lincoln.) Brown left behind a written note: "I John Brown am now quite certain that the crimes of this guilty land will never be purged away, but with Blood. I had . . . vainly flattered myself that without very much bloodshed, it might be done."

During a memorable May 30, 1881 oration at the Fourteenth Anniversary of

Storer College at Harper's Ferry, Frederick Douglass said, "Did John Brown fail? John Brown began the war that ended American slavery and made this a free Republic. His zeal in the cause of my race was far greater than mine. I could live for the slave, but he could die for him."

John Brown's Fort. The federal armory and arsenal would soon become known as John Brown's Fort and became a popular tourist attraction. It has been moved four times: to Chicago for the World's Columbian Exposition in 1891; to the Murphy Farm near Harpers Ferry in 1895; and to the Storer College campus in 1909. In 1968 John Brown's Fort was moved to its present location, where it has been ever since.

On July 14, 1896, during their first National Convention, the National League of Colored Women visited John Brown's Fort. They were the first group known to make such a pilgrimage to this site.

Storer College, a Historically Black College. John Brown's Fort is not the only African-American tourist attraction at Harpers Ferry. Also in the national park is the former campus of Storer College, a historically black college located on Camp Hill. Over an almost ninety-year period, the educational institution that eventually came to be known as Storer College grew from a one-room school for freedmen into a full-fledged, degree-granting college open to all races, creeds, and colors. Frederick Douglass was one of its trustees and used its campus to deliver his famous speech about John Brown on May 30, 1881:

> The true question is, Did John Brown draw his sword against slavery and thereby lose his life in vain? And to this I answer ten thousand times, No! No man fails, or can fail, who so grandly gives himself and all he has to a righteous cause. No man, who in his hour of extremest need, when on his way to meet an ignominious death, could so forget himself as to stop and kiss a little child, one of the hated race for whom he was about to die, could by any possibility fail.

In addition, the Niagara Movement (a forerunner of the NAACP), founded by W.E.B. DuBois and other leading African Americans, chose Storer College for its second national conference in 1906.

Despite the school's history and distinguished graduates—including J. R. Clifford, West Virginia's first black lawyer and owner of the first black newspaper; Howard University professor Coralie Franklin Cook; Joseph Jeffrey Walters, writer of the first African novel published in English, *Guanya Pau;* and Nnamdi Azikiwe, a 1928 graduate who became president of Nigeria—Storer's fate was sealed when the Supreme Court handed down the landmark school desegregation decision of *Brown v. Board of Education of Topeka, Kansas.* The judgment ended federal and state support for Storer College, and in 1955 the college shut down. The National Park Service now uses the remaining buildings as a training facility.

Washington County, Sandy Hook

Washington County is a little bit of a drive from the Washington, D.C., metro area, but a serious student of African-American history will make the trip. John Brown's headquarters at Kennedy's Farm is worth it.

John Brown's Headquarters (Kennedy's Farm)

Harpers Ferry is the logical choice for people looking to explore the history of John Brown's failed attempt to free the slaves of the South, but there is a second location in Maryland that is just as fascinating and just as important to Brown's plan to free the slaves.

Kennedy's Farm in Sandy Hook, Maryland, is the location from which Brown planned his raid of the federal armory and arsenal, a move he hoped would inspire slaves to rebel against their owners. Brown, his children, and his compatriots rented the 194 acres of land and cottage from the estate of Dr. Robert F. Kennedy for three and a half months while they plotted the raid on Harpers Ferry.

The farmhouse and grounds where Brown and his Provisional Army of the United States trained for their first—and only—strike against the slaveholding South are now open for tourists who are interested in how this man and his army planned and lived. Inside, John Brown himself, or at least a realistic plastic mannequin in his likeness, sits at a dining room table, planning the raid, while models of one of his sons and another lieutenant wait in the wings. If the house itself is not open, visitors can peek in the windows to see Brown and the house's interior, and an audio information box on the porch plays tapes with information about the site upon request.

The Planning Stages of John Brown's Raid. Brown assumed a false identity as a New York cattleman named Isaac Smith when he arrived at Sandy

Hook. He was looking for a secluded place where he could raise an army without the neighbors getting suspicious. The Kennedy farmhouse was perfect, considering the amount of land and the fact that Kennedy himself had died a few years earlier. It also sat only five miles north of Harpers Ferry, on the Maryland side of the Potomac.

Brown and his children moved into the house and began their work raising the Provisional Army of the United States. Daughter Annie, sixteen, and daughter-in-law Martha, eighteen, served as cooks and housekeepers for Brown's army, which included Brown's sons Owen, Watson, and Oliver. The women also served as lookouts for inquisitive neighbors and diverted them while the men hid. "When I washed dishes, I stood at the end of the table where I could see out of the window and open door if any one approached the house," Annie wrote in later years. "I was constantly on the lookout while carrying the victuals across the porch, and while I was tidying or sweeping the rooms, and always at my post on the porch when the men were eating. My evenings were spent on the porch or sitting on the stairs watching or listening."

While they were cooped up inside, the men spent their time drilling and reading military manuals. At night, they would exercise, get fresh air, and prepare for battle.

Osborne Perry Anderson. Osborne Perry Anderson described life at Kennedy's Farm in his 1861 book *A Voice from Harper's Ferry: A Narrative of Events at Harper's Ferry; with Incidents Prior and Subsequent to Its Capture by Captain Brown and His Men*:

> Every morning, when the noble old man was at home, he called the family around, read from his Bible, and offered to God most fervent and touching supplications for all flesh; and especially pathetic were his petitions in behalf of the oppressed. I never heard John Brown pray, that he did not make strong appeals to God for the deliverance of the slave. This duty over, the men went to the loft, there to remain all the day long; few only could be seen about, as the neighbors were watchful and suspicious. It was also important to talk but little among ourselves, as visitors to the house might be curious. Besides the daughter and daughter-in-law, who superintended the work, some one or other of the men was regularly detailed to assist in the cooking, washing, and other domestic work. After the ladies left, we did all the work, no one being exempt, because of age or official grade in the organization.

The principal employment of the prisoners, as we severally were when compelled to stay in the loft, was to study Forbes' Manual, and to go through a quiet, though rigid drill, under the training of Capt. Stevens, at some times. At others, we applied a preparation for bronzing our gun barrels—discussed subjects of reform—related our personal history; but when our resources became pretty well exhausted, the ennui from confinement, imposed silence, etc., would make the men almost desperate. At such times, neither slavery nor slaveholders were discussed mincingly. We were, while the ladies remained, often relieved of much of the dullness growing out of restraint by their kindness. As we could not circulate freely, they would bring in wild fruit and flowers from the woods and fields. We were well supplied with grapes, paw-paws, chestnuts, and other small fruit, besides bouquets of fall flowers, through their thoughtful consideration.

During the several weeks I remained at the encampment, we were under the restraint I write of through the day; but at night, we sallied out for a ramble, or to breathe the fresh air and enjoy the beautiful solitude of the mountain scenery around, by moonlight.

This routine continued all through July, August and September, until Brown sent his daughter and daughter in law home and rode off to take the Harper's Ferry arsenal.

Anderson was the only African American to survive the raid, and he was also the only man to write a book containing an eyewitness account of Brown and the raid. After slipping out of Harpers Ferry into Pennsylvania, the freeborn Anderson was hidden by Underground Railroad agents Henry Watson in Chambersburg, William Goodridge in York, and William Still in Philadelphia. He made it to Canada, where he eventually told his tale to Mary Ann Shadd, North America's first African-American newspaperwoman and the editor of the antislavery newspaper the *Provincial Freeman*. The experience led Shadd to serve as the publisher of *A Voice From Harper's Ferry*.

Anderson enlisted with the Union Army in 1864, serving honorably and becoming involved in recruiting other African-American soldiers for the Union. He died at age forty-two and was eulogized in Washington, D.C., in 1872.

Landmark Status at Last. The Kennedy Farm from which Brown launched the raid on Harpers Ferry has always been valued for its place in history. It was purchased in 1950 by the National Negro Elks, who hoped to make it a museum and shrine to honor Brown. However, the Elks were not able to raise enough money, and they sold the Kennedy Farm to Bonnard Morgan in 1966. Finally, a

The Storming of the Engine House at Harpers Ferry
LIBRARY OF CONGRESS, LC-USZ62-126970

The Fate of Participants in the Raid

Osborne Perry Anderson was the only African American still alive at the end of John Brown's raid. Four white men also escaped the assault and were never captured: Brown's son Owen, Charles P. Tidd, Barclay Coppoc, and Francis J. Merriam. The four other African-American raiders died during the assault or were hanged later. John A. Copeland Jr. was hanged along with Shields Green, who had escaped slavery in South Carolina and joined Brown after being introduced to him by Frederick Douglass. The two African Americans killed during the raid were Lewis Leary and Dangerfield Newby, who had been freed by his white master/father, but who was trying to free his enslaved wife and seven children.

private developer and Brown aficionado named South T. Lynn bought the farm in 1972 and restored it to Brown-era appearance, leading the federal government to deem it a National Historic Landmark. *The Kennedy Farm; 2406 Chestnut Grove Road, Sharpsburg, MD. To arrange a tour, write to captain@johnbrown.org.*

The Banneker-Douglass Museum

Annapolis

In addition to being a lovely riverside town, Annapolis is the state capital of
Maryland and one of the most important cities in African-American literature
because of its connection to the famous book *Roots*. It's also home to the U.S.
Naval Academy and the Maryland Statehouse, the oldest continuously used legislative building in the United States.

The Banneker-Douglass Museum

Named after two of the most famous Maryland-born African Americans—mathematician and astronomer Benjamin Banneker and orator and civil rights leader
Frederick Douglass—the Banneker-Douglass Museum is Maryland's official
repository for African-American cultural artifacts. It holds one of the state's
largest collections of art, rare books, artifacts, historical documents, and photographs depicting African-American life in Maryland.

A short walk from the historic Maryland Statehouse in the heart of downtown Annapolis, the Banneker-Douglass Museum is located inside a historical building: the old Mount Moriah African Methodist Episcopal Church. Built in the early 1800s by freed slaves, it became one of the first churches for African Americans in Maryland's capital city. The Victorian Gothic structure was placed on the National Register of Historic Places in 1973 and converted into the Banneker-Douglass Museum in 1984 as Maryland's first state-supported African-American museum.

The original museum could only display rotating exhibits from its collection due to limited space, but in 2006 officials completed a multimillion-dollar, four-story addition to the Banneker-Douglass Museum. The addition doubled its gallery and office space and allowed the museum to host its first permanent exhibit: "Deep Roots, Rising Waters: A History of African Americans in Maryland," an overview of African-American history in Maryland from 1633 to the civil rights movement.

The museum hosts year-round lectures, workshops, performances, and other programs relating to African-American history. The Banneker-Douglass Museum also has a nonlending library where patrons can study photographs, manuscripts, videotapes, and archival materials by appointment.

The Thurgood Marshall Memorial

In 1996 an eight-foot statue of a young Thurgood Marshall was placed in front of the building where Marshall successfully argued in the Maryland Court of Appeals for the admission of Donald Gaines Murray to the University of Maryland Law School. The statue depicts the young lawyer striding out of the building, having taken his first major steps in his lifelong goal to achieve equal justice under law.

The grandson of a slave, Thoroughgood "Thurgood" Marshall became one

Thurgood Marshall
LIBRARY OF CONGRESS, LC-U9-1027B-11

The Thurgood Marshall Memorial

of the best lawyers and judges in American history through his tireless passion for equal justice and civil rights. Born in Baltimore, he attended historically black Lincoln University in Chester County, Pennsylvania, with such luminaries as poet and author Langston Hughes; the future President of Ghana, Kwame Nkrumah; and musician Cab Calloway. Upon graduating Marshall applied to the University of Maryland Law School but was denied admission because he was African American. This was a defining event in his life. After graduating from Howard University Law School, Marshall's first major court case was against the University of Maryland and its racist policy. He successfully sued the university in 1935 and forced the school to admit Murray.

The bronze statue outside the Maryland Statehouse in Lawyers' Mall is not alone. Included in the memorial are three other statues. Sitting on benches, as if waiting for an update from Marshall, are Murray and two African-American children. Murray represents Marshall's first major civil rights victory, while the two

Thurgood Marshall

Marshall continued to blossom after the Murray case, working with the NAACP and winning dozens of Supreme Court cases, including the famous

MORE FACTS

Brown v. Board of Education of Topeka, Kansas, case ending state-sponsored segregation in America's classrooms. He also served as U.S. solicitor general, winning fourteen of the nineteen cases he argued in front of the court on behalf of the government.

In 1954 Marshall became a federal appellate judge of such renown that the Supreme Court never overturned any of his majority opinions, and he was elevated to the high court in 1967. He served as the court's first African-American justice until his retirement in 1991. He died two years later.

Although Marshall has been memorialized in several ways (including the renaming of the Baltimore-Washington International Airport after him), the Thurgood Marshall Memorial takes us back to his beginning as a young lawyer trying to fight state-sponsored segregation.

African-American children represent his greatest victory in *Brown v. Board of Education of Topeka, Kansas.* Written on the ground around the statue is the following statement:

> Thurgood Marshall's first major victory in his lifelong struggle for equality under the law for all Americans took place in the Maryland Court of Appeals, which then stood near this memorial. In 1935 Marshall successfully argued for the admission of Donald Murray to the University of Maryland School of Law. This was the first step on the road to Brown v. the Board of Education of Topeka in which the United States Supreme Court in 1954 overturned the doctrine of "separate but equal" established by Plessy v. Ferguson (1896). Throughout his life, Thurgood Marshall fought to fulfill the promise held within the quote above the entrance to the United States Supreme Court building in Washington, D.C. "Equal Justice Under Law."

Matthew Alexander Henson Memorial

Matthew Alexander Henson was a man of historic firsts. He is remembered as the first man to reach the North Pole, but he is also the first African-American man to have a memorial sponsored by the state of Maryland.

Born in Nanjemoy, Maryland, on August 8, 1866, and orphaned after the death of his parents, Henson began traveling the world at the age of thirteen. He eventually met up with Navy officer Robert Edwin Peary, and, as Peary's indispensable assistant, he began making attempts to reach the North Pole. The two men worked as a team to become the first men to reach the North Pole. While Peary has been credited since the early 1900s as the first man to have discovered the North Pole, Henson beat him and their four Eskimo guides by forty-five minutes. He greeted Peary from the North Pole on April 6, 1909, with: "I think I'm the first man to sit on top of the world."

It took years for Henson's achievement to be acknowledged by the public, but he was eventually honored along with Peary for reaching what they thought to be the geographic North Pole. (Modern scientists say they didn't actually make it—a fact that wouldn't be known until 1989, when the National Geographic Society concluded that he had made it within five miles of the North Pole.)

Henson died on March 9, 1955, and was buried in New York. In 1959 his birth state honored him by placing a memorial plaque inside the Rotunda of the Maryland State House to ensure that the great explorer's accomplishments would never be forgotten.

In 1988 Henson's body was moved to Arlington National Cemetery, the final resting place of the country's greatest heroes. (His grave can be found in Section 8, Special Lot S-15.) Henson also was the great-grandnephew of Josiah Henson, an escaped slave whose memoir is believed to have been Harriet Beecher Stowe's inspiration for *Uncle Tom's Cabin*. *Maryland State House; 100 State Circle, Annapolis, MD; 410-974-2804.*

The Kunta Kinte-Alex Haley Memorial

With the publication of his Pulitzer Prize–winning book *Roots*, writer Alex Haley took the entire world on a powerful journey; he brought readers through the struggles and triumphs of Africans brought to America as slaves, as well as the struggles of their descendants. Millions of people still remember the first time

The Kunta Kinte-Alex Haley Memorial

they read the book or watched the story retold in the television miniseries (the first consecutive-night miniseries ever to be shown on television), including the arrival of Kunta Kinte at Annapolis Harbor on September 29, 1767, aboard the ship *Lord Ligonier.*

The Kunta Kinte-Alex Haley Memorial in Annapolis Harbor was erected in recognition of this incredible true tale and the masterful storytelling and researching abilities of Haley, a true American craftsman. It is also considered to be the only memorial in the country that commemorates the name of an enslaved African and the location of his arrival in the United States.

The memorial was completed in 2002 and consists of three parts: the Compass Rose, the Story Wall, and the Sculpture Group. The easiest to find is the Sculpture Group, a life-size bronze statue of the late Haley sitting at the edge of Annapolis Harbor reading a book about his family's history to three children: one black, one white, and one Asian. Next to the statues are three bronze plaques, including one from 1981 commemorating Kunta Kinte's arrival in the

United States. (The original plaque commemorating Kunta Kinte's arrival was stolen from Annapolis Harbor within days of its being dedicated in 1981. The plaque in the Sculpture Group is a replacement.)

To Haley's left and along the edge of the city's seawall is the one-hundred-foot Story Wall, which consists of ten bronze plaques bearing words from Haley's most famous work, *Roots*. The final part of the memorial, the Compass Rose, is to Haley's left and across the street. The fourteen-foot bronze center-piece contains a map of the world with Annapolis at its center. Using the Compass Rose, visitors can stand on the map's center and face the direction of their ancestors' homeland.

Baltimore County

Benjamin Banneker has such a connection to the Washington, D.C., area that it would be a shame to pass up seeing his roots in Cantonville in Baltimore County. It's just a short drive from the District of Columbia, and you'll see that it is worth the ride.

Benjamin Banneker Historical Park and Museum, Cantonville

Known around the world as the first African-American scientist and the man who helped lay the foundation for Washington, D.C., mathematician and astronomer Benjamin Banneker's ties are strongest to the District of Columbia's northern neighbor, Maryland.

Banneker's grandfather, Bannaka, was African royalty from the Senegal region of Africa who was captured and sold to America as a slave. Lucky for him, the person who purchased him, an Englishwoman named Molly Welsh, soon freed him—and then married him. Taking on Bannaka's first name as their last name, the family's children settled on a site in Oella, where the Benjamin Banneker Historical Park and Museum now sits. A 142-acre site made up of the original farm purchased by Banneker's father (and later farmed by Banneker himself), the park has several nature trails and walking loops that allow visitors to explore the land where the Bannekers farmed tobacco, wheat, vegetables, and honey. Archeologists and scientists are now combing the park for artifacts in hopes of better understanding and preserving the memory of one of the most brilliant minds of his era.

Inside the museum is a detailed history of Banneker and his times, including a model of a wooden striking clock similar to the one that Banneker invented at age twenty-two with no formal schooling. His skill was such that he was able to create the clock after borrowing, disassembling, and then reassembling a pocket watch. Banneker's wooden clock was so expertly crafted that it continued to strike the hour without fail for more than fifty years. With a borrowed telescope Banneker also crafted the first almanac written by an African American that accurately predicted tides, sunrises, sunsets, and even an eclipse.

From his farm Banneker published *Benjamin Banneker's Almanac* between 1792 and 1797. The museum has several exhibits featuring replica pages from Banneker's handwritten journals, a multimedia display, and a viewing area showing the Ossie Davis movie *The Man Who Loved the Stars.* The park features special programs designed to explore Banneker's history, and it is in the midst of reconstructing Banneker's original cabin so that visitors can experience eighteenth-century life as seen by Benjamin Banneker. *Benjamin Banneker Historical Park and Museum; 300 Oella Avenue,* Cantonville, MD; 410-887-1081.

Baltimore

The closest major city to Washington, D.C., is Baltimore, Maryland, a city with its own African-American history to tell.

Billie Holiday Statue

Although the city of Baltimore is not the first place that comes to mind when people think of iconic jazz great Billie Holiday, the legendary singer grew up and likely gave her first performances on the mean streets of Charm City.

No one knows exactly where Billie Holiday was born in 1915, but as Eleanora Fagan (her real name), she spent much of her troubled and wild early life in East Baltimore. She discovered jazz artists like Louis Armstrong and Bessie Smith while scrubbing floors and running errands for a local bordello. With songs like "God Bless the Child" and "Strange Fruit" (which *Time* magazine named "The Best Song of the Century" in 1999), her sultry, smoky, but tortured voice would make her famous in the nightclubs of Harlem. Her famous and fanciful autobiography, *Lady Sings the Blues,* chronicled in 1956 her difficult childhood and her performances at Baltimore's famous Royal Theatre before her drug addition killed her at age forty-four.

Billie Holiday statue

Billie Holiday Vocal Competition

If you happen to be in Baltimore in early spring, the city puts on a Billie Holiday Vocal Competition for aspiring singers who want to follow in the vocal steps of America's greatest jazz singer. For more information contact the Baltimore Office of Promotion & the Arts; 443-263-4321; www.promotionandarts.com.

Today, across from where the Royal Theatre once stood, "Lady Day" is forever immortalized with an 8½-foot bronze statue near the streets where she spent time as a child. Dedicated in 1985, the statue crafted by Baltimore native and African-American sculptor James Earl Reid shows Holiday in a jazz pose wearing a sultry evening gown with her trademark white gardenias adorning her hair. *Billie Holiday statue; 1300 Pennsylvania Avenue, Baltimore, MD.*

Mother Mary Lange Monument, Oblate Sisters of Providence, and St. Francis Academy

In 2000 the city of Baltimore erected a four-foot-tall memorial honoring Mother Mary Lange and the Oblate Sisters of Providence for their work with children in the city.

Despite the challenges of being a African-American woman living in a slave-holding, sexist, and racist society in 1800s Baltimore, Mother Mary Lange accomplished something that no one had before: the founding of the very first African-American order of Roman Catholic nuns and the creation of the oldest continuously serving school for African-American children. Born as Elizabeth Clarisse Lange in the Caribbean islands (oral tradition has her born in Haiti in the 1780s), she was educated in Cuba and moved with her family to Baltimore in 1813 to live in a community of French-speaking Haitians.

Well-spoken, forceful, and financially independent despite being a black Catholic woman in pre–Emancipation Proclamation America, she saw a need in her community for education. Lange, along with Madeleine Marie Balas, opened up in her home a free school for children, which operated for more than a decade. After being forced to close the school because of financial pressure, Lange was approached by James Whitfield, the archbishop of Baltimore, with an unheard-of opportunity to found a Catholic order of nuns with the goal of educating African-American children. In 1828, along with her friend Marie and two other women, she founded the St. Frances of Rome Academy, the oldest-known African-American school for children, and in 1829 she founded the Oblate Sisters of Providence, the first African-American religious order. Lange became first superior and superior general and took the name Mary.

For years Mother Mary Lange and the Oblate Sisters educated African-American children, took in orphans, and even educated and allowed freed slaves to join their order. This upset several people in Baltimore, where some Catholics were slave owners. After Whitfield died, the new archbishop ordered the sisters to disband and become domestics. Mother Mary refused to disband the order, but they did accept work as housekeepers at St. Mary's Seminary under strict conditions. "As persons of color and religious at the same time, we wish to conciliate these two qualities as not to appear too arrogant nor miss the respect which is due to the state we have embraced and the holy habit we have the honor to wear," Mother Lange wrote to the Rev. Louis Deluol. "Our intention in consenting to your request is not to neglect the religious profession which we have embraced."

Although Mother Mary Lange died in 1882, St. Frances Academy is still going strong in Baltimore as a Catholic high school under the auspices of the Oblate Sisters of Providence. Mother Mary Lange and her work are now getting national attention, more than one hundred years after her death. The Roman Catholic Church is considering making her a saint, and the city of Baltimore has honored her and the order she founded with a memorial. *Mother Mary Lange Monument; George Street off of Pennsylvania Avenue, Baltimore, MD.*

Thurgood Marshall Memorial

Thurgood Marshall's hometown of Baltimore honored the esteemed Supreme Court justice in 1980 by placing an eight-foot-tall statue of him wearing his Supreme Court justice robes in front of the federal courthouse downtown. Small wonder, given Marshall's accomplishments.

Marshall attended Frederick Douglass High School in Baltimore (he

Tributes to Thurgood Marshall

Thurgood Marshall is likely the most honored Supreme Court justice in American history. Here are some recent tributes:

- Maryland's largest airport was recently renamed the Baltimore/ Washington International Thurgood Marshall Airport in his honor.

- The Supreme Court named its new administrative building in Washington, D.C., the Thurgood Marshall Federal Judiciary Center.

- The University of Maryland in College Park has renamed its law library after him.

- Texas Southern University has officially renamed its law school the Thurgood Marshall School of Law.

- Thurgood Marshall College in La Jolla, California, which opened in 1970 as Third College, changed its name to honor Marshall in 1993.

changed his name from Thoroughgood to Thurgood while in elementary school, saying Thoroughgood had too many letters), which was where he first learned the Constitution. (His punishment for misbehaving was to learn the Constitution by heart, and by the time he finished school, he knew it.)

Marshall returned to Baltimore to practice law after finishing Howard University Law School. The very next year, in 1934, NAACP general counsel Charles Houston (the first African American to win a case in front of the Supreme Court) hired Marshall to work for the Baltimore branch of the National Association for the Advancement of Colored People. Four years later, Marshall replaced Houston as the NAACP's chief counsel and director-counsel of the NAACP legal defense and educational fund. As NAACP director/lawyer, he won twenty-nine out of thirty cases he argued in front of the Supreme Court in his fight against segregation. *Thurgood Marshall Memorial; on Pratt Street, outside the Edward A. Garmatz Federal Building and U.S. Courthouse, Baltimore, MD.*

Reginald F. Lewis Museum of Maryland African American History & Culture

The largest museum of African-American history on the East Coast, the Reginald F. Lewis Museum of Maryland African American History & Culture, sits just steps away from the vibrant Inner Harbor neighborhood in the resurgent downtown area of Baltimore. The museum was made possible by an endowment from Reginald Lewis, who was a Baltimore native, a successful African-American businessman, and a partner in the first African-American law firm on Wall Street. Lewis died at age fifty in 1993, but his generosity allowed the museum to open in 2005 with a mission to study, preserve, and promote the contributions that African Americans made to Maryland and the rest of the country.

Using video, audio, and the printed word, permanent exhibits like "Building Maryland, Building America" and "The Strength of the Mind" on the museum's third floor tout the contributions of Maryland's African-American population to

The Reginald F. Lewis Museum of Maryland African American History & Culture, the largest museum of African-American history on the East Coast

American culture, science, labor, music, and art. Special exhibits focusing on art, photography, and other disciplines shine on the museum's second floor.

Scattered throughout the museum are artifacts, touch-screen computers, and listening stations that let tourists explore African-American history in more depth and listen to oral histories of Maryland's African Americans. A two-hundred-seat theater/auditorium, an oral history recording studio, and a resource center allow the museum to put on periodic theatrical, dance, and musical performances, as well as lectures, panel discussions, and programs on Maryland history and genealogy. *The Reginald F. Lewis Museum of Maryland African American History & Culture; 830 E Pratt Street, Baltimore, MD; 443-263-1800.*

National Great Blacks in Wax Museum

Billing itself as one of America's top-ten African-American history attractions, the National Great Blacks in Wax Museum uses lifelike wax replicas to take visitors on an unflinching tour through African-American history, from ancient Egypt to modern days. Like other famous wax museums, the National Great

National Great Blacks in Wax Museum

Blacks in Wax Museum has dozens of depictions of famous and not-so-famous (but historically important) African Americans in wax. What sets this museum apart are two exhibits: "The Slave Ship Experience," a life-size depiction of the interior of a slave ship, with scenes in wax of the horrible cruelty that male and female African slaves suffered during the crossing of the Atlantic Ocean to the United States; and "Lynching: A Legacy of Terror," a display of the bloody remains of a southern lynching of male and female African Americans. (WARN-ING: Several of the slave ship and lynching exhibits depict bloody and realistic acts of cruelty, and parents of young children should be advised that the scenes are very realistic and potentially upsetting.) Both exhibits are located in cramped underground quarters off the main floor, allowing those who choose not to view these scenes to skip them and view exhibits like "Black Youth in the Struggle," "A Journey to Freedom," "Blacks in the Military," and "Modern Civil Rights Era" instead. Founded in 1983 the museum is in the midst of a campaign to expand from its current 15,000 square feet to more than 120,000 square feet of interactive exhibitions. *National Great Blacks in Wax Museum; 1601 E North Avenue #3, Baltimore, MD; 410-563-3404.*

Frederick Douglass-Isaac Myers Maritime Park

African Americans played a large part in Maryland's naval tradition, as evidenced by the recent opening of the Frederick Douglass-Isaac Myers Maritime Park. The park is a re-creation of the Chesapeake Marine Railway and Dry Dock Company, the first African-American-owned marine railway and shipyard in the United States.

Visitors can tour a museum in the historic Sugar House, the oldest remaining industrial building in Baltimore's Inner Harbor. Along a harborside promenade there are exhibits where visitors and students can watch artisans restore nineteenth-century sailing vessels. There is also a 1912 vintage marine railway that can handle wooden and historic ships weighing up to one hundred tons.

The new park is named after Frederick Douglass, who lived in Baltimore and worked in the maritime trades, and Isaac Myers, who founded the shipyard and the first black maritime unions.

Isaac Myers and the Chesapeake Marine Railway and Dry Dock Company. The Chesapeake Marine Railway and Dry Dock Company was

founded just west of the new park and is notable for setting a new Baltimore standard by employing African Americans without discrimination. Before the Civil War, Baltimore had one of the largest free African-American populations. Many of these African Americans worked in shipbuilding, but they were pushed out after the war to make room for growing numbers of white workers. In fact, following the Civil War, Irish and German workers banded together and told shipyard owners they would not work with blacks, and violent clashes ensued.

Faced with such discrimination, Isaac Myers and fourteen other investors decided to open their own shipyard. The Chesapeake Marine Railway and Dry Dock Company was founded in 1868 by Myers, with money from Douglass and others, to employ black shipbuilders who had lost their jobs.

Douglass was willing to help because he had worked as a caulker in the 1830s. He used that trade to earn a living after escaping from slavery (before he achieved fame as an abolitionist and speaker). He also purchased his first book a block away from the new park and met his first wife in the nearby Fell's Point community.

Myers, meanwhile, was a free African-American caulker who was so skillful that by age twenty he was supervising caulking on Baltimore's largest ships. He went into business for himself in the 1860s, eventually opening up his own grocery store and learning the value of owning his own business. Myers went back into ship caulking in 1865, just in time to see white workers attempt to push African-American workers out of the business. To fight this, Myers and his group of investors decided to open their own company, but white landowners in the Baltimore harbor refused to sell a shipyard to them. The group eventually was able to obtain a yard with the help of a sympathetic white intermediary, businessman William Applegarth, who leased lot 42 on Philpot Street, two parcels with water frontage, in the name of the "John Smith Company" in 1866. The John Smith Company was chartered two years later as the Chesapeake Marine Railway and Dry Dock Company.

The Chesapeake Marine Railway and Dry Dock Company was one of the most successful companies in the Baltimore harbor. Hiring experienced black and white workers, the company's success in both caulking and repair led boat owners from around the Chesapeake region to send their ships to the yard. That business led to a number of government contracts, and the success allowed the Chesapeake Marine Railway and Dry Dock Company pay off its debts in five years.

Although the shipyard's charter included a provision that the company was to exist for forty years, due to a misunderstanding, the lease expired and was not renewed in 1884. The company ceased operations that year.

The Colored National Labor Union. Isaac Myers didn't just spearhead the creation of the first African-American-owned shipyard. He also led the very first national labor union for African-American workers. Myers created the Colored National Labor Union in 1869, making it the first large-scale national entity of black workers. The Colored National Labor Union disintegrated within a few years; but while Myers was its leader, the all-white National Labor Union opened its conference to persons of all color in 1869. Myers was invited to speak at that convention and was one of nine blacks that attended the convention. Myers would later go on to tour the country, talking about labor rights and politics before coming home to Baltimore, where he died in 1891. *Frederick Douglass-Isaac Myers Maritime Park; 1417 Thames Street, Baltimore, MD; 410-685-0295 ext. 252.*

Other Places of Interest

Checking out these other sites will take a real time commitment if you're starting out in the District, but if you have time and transportation, they're well worth the drive.

Harriet Tubman Sites

Harriet Tubman Historical Marker, Bucktown. Harriet Tubman could easily be considered the most remarkable American woman who ever lived. After escaping slavery in Maryland, she returned to the South to become the most successful conductor of the Underground Railroad, a network of antislave activists who ushered escaped slaves to safety up North. Historians have said she led as many as three hundred slaves from as far south as South Carolina to freedom in the northern states and Canada before the Civil War.

Tubman, who was born Araminta Ross (Harriet was her mother's name and Tubman was her married name), lived the early portion of her life as a slave in Bucktown, Maryland, on the Edward Brodess plantation with her brothers and sisters. Near the plantation is the Bucktown store, which history says was the site of the first recorded instance of Tubman's defiance. A slave overseer ordered Tubman to help him subdue an escaped slave in the store, but she refused. As the

Full-length portrait of a young Harriet Tubman
LIBRARY OF CONGRESS, LC-USZ62-7816

An elderly Harriet Tubman, probably at her home in Auburn, New York
LIBRARY OF CONGRESS, LC-DIG-pmsca-02909

slave rushed for the door, Tubman blocked the overseer to facilitate the slave's successful escape. She paid a heavy price, though. The enraged overseer picked up a two-pound weight and hurled it at the escaping slave. It hit Harriet in the head instead. The crushing blow incapacitated her for months, leaving her with an ugly scar on her forehead and sudden, unexpected sleeping fits for the rest of her life. A recent biographer, Kate Clifford Larson, wrote in her book *Bound for the Promised Land: Harriet Tubman: Portrait of an American Hero* that Tubman's "sleeping spells, periods of semi-consciousness," were caused by temporal lobe epilepsy from the injury.

Edward Brodess died in 1849 and left his slaves to his wife, who planned to sell Tubman and the other slaves to the Deep South to make some money. The time had come to leave, Tubman thought. One night she headed north by

Harriett Tubman

During the Civil War, Harriet Tubman worked for the United States as a nurse, spy, and scout. In addition, she led a Union Army attack on the Con-

federacy in South Carolina, disrupting Southern supply lines by destroying bridges and railroads. Reporting on the raid to Secretary of War Edwin Stanton, Brig. Gen. Rufus Saxton said, "This is the only military command in American history wherein a woman, black or white, led the raid and under whose inspiration it was originated and conducted." After the Civil War, she became an advocate for civil rights and women's rights and received numerous honors for her work as the "Moses of her people."

following the Greenbriar Swamp along the edge of the Brodess fields. Traveling by night and hiding during the day, she made it across the Mason-Dixon line to Philadelphia.

The historical marker honoring Harriet Tubman sits next to a highway that runs through the former location of the Brodess farm, which is now private farmland. *Harriet Tubman Historical Marker; one and a half miles down Greenbriar Road, on the left, Cambridge, MD.*

Harriet Tubman Memorial Garden, Cambridge. Six miles away from Bucktown is the town of Cambridge, where visitors can find several tributes to the life of Harriet Tubman. One of the most prominent is the Harriet Tubman Memorial Garden, which was opened and dedicated in May 2000. Nestled in a prominent spot next to a portion of Highway 50 that is dedicated to Tubman, the garden provides a place of serenity and peace for visitors to learn about Tubman and her work as a conductor of the Underground Railroad. Informational panels scattered throughout the garden tell the story of the Underground Railroad and Tubman's life, including the little-known fact that she was born a free woman.

Tubman's mother, Harriet Green, was given by her master to a relative under the condition that Green was supposed to serve this woman until Green's forty-fifth birthday. The woman died, which by law made Harriet Green a free woman. However, like many slaves, Harriet Green could not read or write, and no one informed her of her freedom. As a result, she and her children, including Tubman, remained slaves until Tubman freed them by way of a daring escape on the Underground Railroad.

Benches are provided throughout the Harriet Tubman Memorial Garden for visitors to contemplate the risks that Tubman, escaped slaves, and their supporters took for freedom. *Harriet Tubman Memorial Garden; Route 50, eastbound side at Washington Street, Cambridge, MD.*

The Harriet Tubman Coalition and Underground Railroad Gift Shop, Cambridge. The town of Cambridge has honored Harriet Tubman by hosting the state's only museum dedicated to its most famous African-American woman. Open to visitors by appointment, the Harriet Tubman Coalition and Underground Railroad Gift Shop features rare photographs of Tubman, books about the Underground Railroad, and exhibits on Tubman's activities in the Cambridge area. Some of the exhibits include a letter from Frederick Douglass to Tubman and maps of some of the routes Tubman used to lead slaves to freedom in Canada and the northern states. Also not to be missed is an in-depth explanation of Tubman's final years as a woman's rights activist and founder of a home for aged blacks in Auburn, New York.

Despite all of her work, Tubman died in poverty in New York after the military refused to give her a pension for her service in the Army. Lawmakers and Tubman supporters to this day are trying to force Congress to acknowledge that Tubman should have been paid a full military pension for her work for the Union troops.

Frederick Douglass Birthplace Marker, Tuckahoe

Almost hidden in the green trees near a bridge crossing the Tuckahoe River sits a humble sign marking the birthplace of one of the greatest African-American thinkers and abolitionists, Frederick Douglass. The state of Maryland put the marker close to a bridge dedicated in his name, which is somewhere near where Douglass was born. Although the exact location of Douglass's birthplace is not known, historians think it was an area about six miles away from the marker, and Douglass himself thought he had found his birthplace at that spot. In the

1980 book *Young Frederick Douglass: The Maryland Years,* Dickson J. Preston describes a trip Douglass made to the spot:

> Frederick and Louis Freeman, who had been a slave on this farm when it was owned by Aaron's Grandson, John P. Anthony, studied the lay of the land. Where a deep, curving gully ran up toward the road from Tuckahoe Creek, Freeman pointed out the spot known in his time as "Aunt Bettie's lot." It looked right, and Frederick, searching his memory, recalled a big cedar tree that should be a little deeper in the woods, near the edge of the ravine. He plunged into the underbrush for a look.
>
> The tree was there, and Frederick solemnly declared he had found the exact spot where he was born.

Douglass was born Frederick Augustus Washington Bailey. The son of a slave, Douglass never knew who his father was, but he speculated it was his mother's white master, Captain Anthony. Beaten unmercifully because of his reputation as a defiant slave, he escaped to freedom in New York City from Baltimore, Maryland, with the help of a woman named Anna Murray, who would eventually become his wife. With the help of abolitionists, he then moved to New Bedford, Massachusetts, where he took the name Frederick Douglass. He then began speaking on the evils of slavery in America and England, and his autobiography, *Narrative of the Life of Frederick Douglass: An American Slave,* made him famous.

Douglass had to flee fugitive-slave catchers in the North because of his fame. He traveled to England, where he purchased his freedom for $711.16. Returning to America as a free man, Douglass convinced Abraham Lincoln to allow blacks to fight in the Union Army during the Civil War, leading to the formation of the famed 54th and 55th Massachusetts regiments, in which two of his sons served. After the war and the assassination of Lincoln, Douglass spent the rest of his life as an orator, writer, government official, American ambassador, businessman, and agent for social change advocating for freedom and equality for African Americans. He died in February 1895, but not before inspiring generations of Americans with his ideas of self-determination, equal rights, and the fulfillment of the American dream of personal success.

Frederick Douglass Birthplace Marker; Maryland Route 328, at the south end of the Tuckahoe River Bridge, Easton, MD.

DISCOVERING BLACK HISTORY IN VIRGINIA

Arlington

The Marine Corps War Memorial (Iwo Jima Memorial)

One of the most awe-inspiring memorials overlooking the nation's capital is the Marine Corps War Memorial, better known to most people as the Iwo Jima Memorial. Designed by Horace W. Peaslee, it was officially dedicated by President Dwight D. Eisenhower on November 10, 1954, as a monument not only to the Marines who fought on Iwo Jima but to all Marines who ever put their lives on the line for their country.

The bronze memorial re-creates a Pulitzer Prize–winning photograph of Marines raising a flag during their storming of the tiny Pacific island of Iwo Jima during World War II. Six thirty-two-foot-high bronze figures are shown erecting a sixty-foot flagpole from which an American flag flies twenty-four hours a day. The figures are set on the summit of a rock slope made of rough Swedish granite. Written in gold on the granite is a list of every major Marine Corps battle. There are also two inscriptions. The first honors all Marines: "In honor and in memory of the men of the United States Marine Corps who have given their lives to their country since November 10, 1775." The second honors the Battle of Iwo Jima by quoting the World War II tribute from Fleet Adm. Chester W. Nimitz to the men fighting on the island: "Uncommon Valor was a Common Virtue."

Iwo Jima was one of the few Pacific islands still controlled by the Japanese in February 1945. But that island was crucial to American plans to win the war,

Marine Corps War Memorial (Iwo Jima Memorial)

and the decision was made to take it from the Japanese no matter what. The Marines landed on Iwo Jima on February 19, 1945, after three days of American bombing of the Japanese positions on the island. The main goal for the invading Marines was to capture Mount Suribachi, an extinct volcano that forms the narrow southern tip of the island and rises 550 feet to dominate the area.

By the morning of February 23, the Marines had started climbing to the top of Mount Suribachi while under fire from the Japanese. Despite resistance, by midmorning a small American flag was flying from the top of the mountain, inspiring the troops who were still fighting around the island. By the afternoon, when the mountain was cleared of all enemy resistance, a larger flag was raised by five Marines and a Navy hospital corpsman: Sgt. Michael Strank, Cpl. Harlon H. Block, Pfc. Franklin R. Sousley, Pfc. Rene A. Gagnon, Pfc. Ira Hayes, and PhM. 2/c John H. Bradley, USN. Associated Press photographer Joe Rosenthal got there as the Marines were taking down the first flag and raising the second. Lifting his camera, he framed the larger flag being raised by the Marines and snapped his Pulitzer Prize–winning photograph.

However, just because the flag was raised on Mount Suribachi didn't mean the battle was over. The battle for Iwo Jima would rage on for more than a month and become America's costliest battle in the Pacific. Iwo Jima was the only major battle in the entire Pacific Campaign where American casualties surpassed Japanese fatalities. And the toll of the dead—6,821 Americans, 5,931 of them Marines—accounted for almost a third of all Marine losses in World War II.

African-American Participation in Iwo Jima. The Battle of Iwo Jima and the flag-raising on Mount Suribachi have been recorded in books, photographs, and movies like *Sands of Iwo Jima* and *Flags of Our Fathers,* but the role of African Americans is often glossed over.

Blacks have been Marines since the corps was formed during the Revolutionary War. The Second Continental Congress founded the Marine Corps on November 10, 1775. A Wilmington, Delaware, slave, John Martin, who was also known as Keto, was recruited by Capt. Miles Pennington, Marine officer of the Continental brig *Reprisal,* in April 1776 and died for his country the next year when the *Reprisal* sank in a gale. Two other blacks, Isaac Walker and a man known as Orange, also enlisted at Philadelphia's Tun Tavern, the recruiting headquarters for the new Marine Corps. These men served under Capt. Robert Mullan, the owner of the tavern, and they crossed the Delaware River with General George Washington on Christmas Eve 1776. According to *The Right to Fight: African-American Marines in World War II* by Bernard C. Nalty, Walker and Orange also fought the British at Princeton. After the Revolutionary War was won, however, blacks were banned from serving in integrated units in the military until right before World War II.

Montford Point Marines. The Marine Corps was the last American military service to desegregate, with the corps beginning its recruitment of African-American enlistees a year after President Franklin D. Roosevelt's 1941 order requiring the military to accept all recruits regardless of race. But instead of integrating the corps by allowing African Americans to train at the Parris Island, South Carolina, and San Diego boot camps, the Marine Corps sent its

The Montford Point Marines Memorial at Arlington National Cemetery

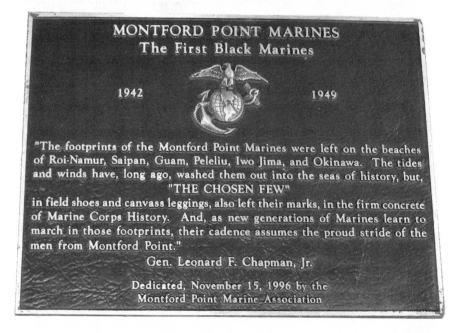

MONTFORD POINT MARINES
The First Black Marines

1942   1949

"The footprints of the Montford Point Marines were left on the beaches
of Roi-Namur, Saipan, Guam, Peleliu, Iwo Jima, and Okinawa. The tides
and winds have, long ago, washed them out into the seas of history, but,
"THE CHOSEN FEW"
in field shoes and canvass leggings, also left their marks, in the firm concrete
of Marine Corps History. And, as new generations of Marines learn to
march in those footprints, their cadence assumes the proud stride of the
men from Montford Point."

Gen. Leonard F. Chapman, Jr.

Dedicated, November 15, 1996 by the
Montford Point Marine Association

African-American enlistees to Camp Montford Point, now known as Camp Lejeune, in North Carolina. Camp Montford Point would become the recruitment and advanced training facility for all African-American Marine enlistees from 1942 through 1949, when segregated units would be dropped. The Marines who went through this camp became known as the Montford Point Marines.

African Americans on Iwo Jima. By 1945 there were more than eight hundred African-American Marines on Iwo Jima for the monthlong assault. They "ferried ammunition and equipment from supply ships in transport areas offshore to the beach. They also evacuated casualties from the beaches. They constructed and repaired airfields even before the fighting ended as the island bases nearest Japan were the final steppingstone to the heart of Japan," according to the 2005 book *Fighting for America: Black Soldiers—The Unsung Heroes of World War II* by Christopher Moore.

The African-American Marines on Iwo Jima didn't just serve in support roles—they also fought the Japanese. When Japanese counterattacks penetrated to the beach areas, the African-American Marines dropped their cargo and engaged in well-disciplined fire. One Montford Point Marine, Thomas McPhatter, said African-American Marines were right behind the invading Marines when they attacked Iwo Jima, despite being forced to serve in supply roles. "As troops moved up, we moved right behind them," McPhatter indicated in the 2004 book *We Were There: Voice of African American Veterans, from World War II to the War in Iraq* by Yvonne Latty and Ron Tarver. "At night, you couldn't tell who was who. The Japanese would dress up like Marines. They would take the uniforms right off the dead Marines and they'd come right into your area and the only way to protect yourself was by using a password. If you didn't get the password right we'd start shooting."

The 8th Field Depot (8th Ammunition Company, 33rd, 34th, and 36th Marine Depot Companies) was cited with the rest of the support troops of the V Amphibious Corps in the Navy Commendation for their part in the furious monthlong battle. Privates James M. Whitlock and James Davis also earned the Bronze Star for "heroic achievement."

Thomas McPhatter and the Flag-Raising. African Americans were indeed involved in the Battle of Iwo Jima, and it was because of African American Thomas McPhatter that the flag-raising happened on Mount Suribachi. The famous flag-raising that was the inspiration for the Iwo Jima Memorial took place only because the Marines were able to plant a small flag on top of Mount Suribachi earlier in the day. The Marines had attached a small flag to a piece of pipe and hoisted it up so everyone could see the gains the Marines had made. The Americans thus claimed ownership of the ground. Staff Sergeant Louis R. Lowery captured the image of this event while working for the Marine magazine *Leathernecks*. McPhatter said he was present for the flag-raising. "The man who put the first flag up on Iwo Jima got a piece of pipe from me to put the flag up on," he told *The Guardian* newspaper.

Once the flag was up on McPhatter's pole, a Marine commander decided that he wanted a larger flag on top of Mount Suribachi. The original flag was taken down and a larger flag was raised. It was this second flag-raising that Joe Rosenthal captured and that won the 1945 Pulitzer Prize for photography.

Women in Military Service for America Memorial

Guarding the gates of Arlington National Cemetery is the Women in Military Service for America Memorial, the only major national memorial in the United States dedicated to all of the women who have served in the armed forces.

Located at the ceremonial entrance to Arlington National Cemetery (the ceremonial gateway was never completely finished despite being dedicated in 1932), the Women's Memorial officially opened to the public on October 20, 1997. With exhibits detailing the contributions of American women to the armed forces from the Revolutionary War through the War on Terror, the Women's Memorial also honors the long history of African-American women in America's armed conflicts. From Mammy Kate Heard, who rescued the governor of Georgia from the British in the Revolutionary War, to Army Sgt. Danyell Wilson, who became the first African-American woman assigned the duty of guarding the Tomb of the Unknowns (better known to most people as the Tomb of the Unknown Soldiers) at Arlington National Cemetery in 1997, African-American women have always been there for their country when it was time for battle.

Black Women in the Civil War. Black women have officially been part of the military since the Civil War, when four thousand black women were employed by the Women's Nurses for the Union and at least nine black women served on the Navy Hospital ship *Red Rover*. We even know the names of the women on the *Red Rover:* Betsey Young, Ann Stokes, Sarah Kinno, Ellen Campbell, Alice Kennedy, Lucinda Jenkins, Margaret Jackson, Nancy Buel, and Sally Bohannon.

Cathay Williams, Buffalo Soldier. On November 15, 1866, the first African-American woman to be documented as a member of the Army was "William Cathay," who signed up to become a member of the 38th U.S. Infantry (better known as the Buffalo Soldiers). Of course, very few people know that "William Cathay" was actually Cathay Williams, a former house slave and cook who wanted to be in the Army. "I wanted to make my own living and not be dependent on relations or friends," Williams told the *St. Louis Daily Times* for a January 2, 1876, article. "Soon after I joined the army, I was taken with the small-pox and was sick at a hospital across the river from St. Louis, but as soon as I got well I joined my company in New Mexico. I was as that paper says, I was never put in the guard house, no bayonet was ever put to my back. I carried my musket and did guard and other duties."

Williams didn't get caught until she was ready to get out of the Army. "I played sick, complained of pains in my side, and rheumatism in my knees. The post surgeon found out I was a woman and I got my discharge," she said in the *Times* article.

Williams now has the honor of being the only documented female Buffalo Soldier and the only documented African-American woman who served in the U.S. Army prior to 1948, when women were officially allowed to join.

There are several exhibits in the Women's Memorial to commemorate brave African-American women soldiers that should not be missed.

Sarah Keys Evans and Dovey Johnson Roundtree. On display at the Women's Memorial Education Center is a plaque honoring Army veterans Sarah Keys Evans and Dovey Johnson Roundtree, who fought not only *for* their country but also *in* their country in the war for civil rights. Despite great personal risk, Evans and Roundtree challenged the South's Jim Crow laws and brought about the Interstate Commerce Commission's decision to strike down the "separate but equal" doctrine in interstate public bus transportation.

Keys was a private in the Army heading home to Washington, North Carolina, in 1952 when a bus driver decided that she should move to the back of the bus to allow a white Marine to move forward. Keys, who was wearing her Army uniform, said no. Keys said in a 2005 interview with the *New York Daily News* that she remembers the bus driver standing in the door, calling a bus number, and saying, "everyone but that woman should get on the other bus." "A soldier offered to carry my bags for me," she said. "But when I got to the other bus the driver would not take my ticket." When she asked why, two policemen "grabbed [her], one on each shoulder, and told [her she was] going to jail."

Keys was arrested for disorderly conduct, taken to jail, and held overnight as the bus moved on. She was fined $25 and was not released from her cell until 3:00 p.m. the next day. Angered by this treatment, Keys and her family sued. After losing the first round in court, they dropped their lawyer and hired the NAACP's recommended lawyer, a woman named Dovey Johnson Roundtree.

Roundtree knew how difficult dealing with segregation and sexism could be. She and thirty-six other black women were among the first class of women commissioned as officers in the Women's Army Auxiliary Corps on August 29, 1942. At that time, African-American women were still segregated in an all-female unit. They were forced to serve in separate units, live in separate quarters, and eat at separate tables. Despite these difficulties, Roundtree and more than 6,500 other black women served in the WAAC/WAC during World War II.

Keys and Roundtree took their case to the Interstate Commerce Commission, saying that because of the North Carolina Coach Company, Keys suffered discrimination, undue and unreasonable prejudice, and false arrest and imprisonment on the basis of race and color. On November 25, 1955, the ICC ruled that the North Carolina Coach Company was wrong. The ruling outlawed racial discrimination on buses engaged in interstate travel. Five days later a woman named Rosa Parks refused to give up her seat on an Alabama bus, igniting the modern civil rights movement.

The Women's Memorial also has an exhibit featuring African-American women during the Korean War, the first conflict where African Americans were not forced to serve in segregated units.

Arlington National Cemetery

Arlington National Cemetery is our nation's most hallowed burial ground. It is the final resting place for thousands of American heroes and it is one of the most popular tourist sites in the Washington, D.C., area. It is also a fully operational cemetery controlled by the U.S. Army, and it conducts more than 6,300 burials

The Tomb of the Unknown Soldiers at Arlington National Cemetery

each year. Currently, more than 300,000 people are buried at Arlington National Cemetery, making it the second-largest national cemetery in the United States (the largest of the 130 national cemeteries is the Calverton National Cemetery on Long Island).

Arlington National Cemetery was established by Brig. Gen. Montgomery C. Meigs, who first started using the grounds on June 15, 1864. He established the site as a military cemetery to ensure that Robert E. Lee and his family, who had long owned the property as a private plantation but sold it to the U.S. government after the war, would never want to come back.

While the most popular sites at Arlington National Cemetery are the burial site of assassinated president John F. Kennedy and the Tomb of the Unknown Soldiers, there are quite a few African-American history sites for visitors to peruse at this location if they are lucky enough to know about them.

Famous African Americans Buried at Arlington National Cemetery

Army Maj. Alexander T. Augusta, who became the first black surgeon in the Army during the Civil War.

Twenty-two African-American sailors who died when the battleship *Maine* was attacked and sank off of Cuba in 1898.

Charles Young, the first black to reach the rank of Army colonel. Young is one of only ten people whose memorial service was held in the cemetery's Memorial Amphitheater.

Cpl. Freddie Stowers, the only African American to earn a Medal of Honor for World War I action.

Benjamin O. Davis of the Tuskegee Airmen. Davis was the first African-American general in the regular armed forces.

Dorie Miller, a sailor aboard the USS *Arizona*. Miller shot down four enemy airplanes at Pearl Harbor.

Roscoe Robinson Jr., the first African-American four-star general in the Army.

Medgar Evers, the civil rights leader who was assassinated in Mississippi in June 1963.

Matthew Alexander Henson, the first man to reach the North Pole.

Air Force Gen. Daniel "Chappie" James, who was the first African-American four-star general in the American military.

Joe Lewis, the heavyweight boxing champion who held the world championship longer than any other boxer.

Thurgood Marshall, the first African-American Supreme Court justice.

There are thousands of other African Americans buried in Arlington National Cemetery, all deserving our respect for the sacrifices they made for our country.

James Parks, Grave Digger. Even the early stages of Arlington National Cemetery's development have African-American connections. The very first graves in the cemetery were dug by James Parks, a former slave at Arlington House.

Parks, who lived his entire life at Arlington House (the plantation home of George Washington Parke Custis, the stepson of George Washington and of Robert E. Lee, who came to live at Arlington House through his marriage to Custis's daughter, Mary Anna) and the surrounding grounds, is also the only person buried at Arlington National Cemetery who was born on the property. Born in 1843, Parks served as a field slave at Arlington House and went to work for the Union Army on the estate grounds once the Civil War started, doing odd jobs and helping to build the forts on the Potomac River. When Montgomery Meigs began using Arlington House as a cemetery, Parks was the first to begin digging the graves and burying the dead.

When Parks died in 1929, the secretary of war made an exception to policy, and Parks was buried at Arlington Cemetery in Section 15, grave 2.

The Integration of Arlington National Cemetery. It wasn't until after World War II that America started treating all races equally in Arlington National Cemetery. In 1948 President Harry S. Truman ordered the "equality of treatment and opportunity for all persons in the armed services without regard to race, color, religion, or national origin," and the nation's national cemeteries immediately discontinued burial segregation.

The Custis Plantation

The entire site occupied by Arlington National Cemetery can be considered an African-American history site, in view of the efforts slaves put into it for its original owner, George Washington Parke Custis (the grandson of Martha Washington from her first marriage and adopted ward of George Washington). The cemetery occupies just over half of the 1,100 acres of the original Arlington plantation owned by Custis.

Custis wanted a grand house that would overlook the District of Columbia. He sought a place where he could build a memorial to his famous grandfather, so he purchased the land where Arlington National Cemetery sits, and in 1802 he authorized the construction of Arlington House, the grand mansion that sits on top of the hill to this day.

This 1864 photograph shows a group of men, some Union soldiers (including African Americans), in front of Arlington House, Robert E. Lee's former home. The home was taken over by Union forces in 1864, and it later became a memorial site.
LIBRARY OF CONGRESS, LC-DIG-ppmsca-07322

African-American Work on the Custis Plantation.

As was the custom at the time, Custis hired a white architect to design what he wanted, and he forced his slaves to build Arlington House for free.

Records show that Custis owned more than two hundred slaves, and of that number, more than sixty-three lived and worked at Arlington House; those slaves were the ones to dig the red clay soil from the property to make the bricks used at Arlington House. They also gathered shells from the Potomac River to make the stucco used in the walls and exterior of the house. Additionally, they cleared the forest around the house to find timber for the interior flooring and supports.

Unfortunately, there is little else to tell us what type of work the slaves did on the actual construction of Arlington House. What we do know, however, is that the slaves didn't get to enjoy the fine work they did on Arlington House. Most were relegated to living in log cabins on the property that they were forced to construct themselves. None of these cabins remain, but some of the living quarters for the slaves who worked inside Arlington House still exist and are available for viewing.

Slave Quarters at Arlington House. Only two of the slave quarters for house slaves at Arlington House still exist. Each building has three rooms and is supported on a stone foundation. The walls are rough stucco and have Greek Revival architectural details.

Records show that the North Slave Quarters housed four slaves: the carriage driver and his son and the plantation cook and his assistant. The South Slave Quarters housed Mrs. Custis's personal maid, her maid's husband, and their eight children, as well as other slaves who worked in the Custis household.

Robert E. Lee and the Custis Slaves. The Custises kept their slaves in Arlington House for their entire lifetime but promised them their freedom after the Custises died. When Custis passed away in 1857, the new master of the estate, Robert E. Lee—the man who would go on to become the famous Confederate general—took over Arlington House because he was married to Custis's daughter, Mary Ann Randolph Custis.

Paradoxically, Lee officially freed all the slaves at Arlington House on December 29, 1862. Of course, that was one year after he left Arlington House to go to Richmond, Virginia, to accept command of the Virginia militia for the Civil War. By that time the Union Army had moved into Arlington House.

Jim Parks, one of the slaves who lived his entire life on the grounds of Arlington House, said the slaves knew about the Custises' promise. "Maj. Custis left his will in 1857 sayin' we was to be free in five years—everyone, from the cradle up, was to be given $50 and be free," Parks said, according to Arlington National Cemetery's Historical Information Web site. "Col. Lee was to administer the estate, but when the five years were up, they (Union soldiers) were here, and there wasn't no estate; but Col. Lee give us our freedom."

Selina Gray and George Washington's Memorabilia. The federal government eventually seized Arlington House and the surrounding estate and began ransacking the house, including the valuable George Washington memorabilia. The memorabilia would have been lost forever if not for one of the former slaves at Arlington House.

When Lee's family left Arlington House, Mrs. Lee gave the keys of the estate to the chief house slave, Selina Gray, and entrusted her with what possessions were left. When Selina Gray discovered what the Union soldiers were doing, she ordered them "not to touch any of Mrs. Lee's things" and alerted Union general Irvin McDowell to the Washington heirlooms. Through Selina Gray's efforts, many of the Washington pieces were saved for posterity.

Freedman's Village

In addition to using Arlington House and its grounds as a garrison, in 1863 the federal government turned part of the grounds that now comprise Arlington National Cemetery into a self-sustaining village, called the Freedman's Village, for former slaves.

Freedman's Village, Arlington, Virginia

LIBRARY OF CONGRESS, LC-B18184 B1163

LIBRARY OF CONGRESS, LC-USZ62-117892

Historians suspect that this village was located in what is now the southern section of Arlington National Cemetery (Sections 8, 47, and 25) along Eisenhower Drive. More than one hundred former slaves, including some of Robert E. Lee's slaves, settled here and began to work. The slaves became known as "contraband," a term linked with Union major general Benjamin F. Butler. Since Southerners considered slaves property, Butler reasoned that slaves who were freed by the Union Army or who made it up through the Confederate lines to the North would be considered spoils of war for the United States.

The freed slaves paid $10 a month to live in Freedman's Village. The money went toward rent and maintenance fees. Originally, Freedman's Village was run by the Union Army, which was more concerned with winning the Civil War than taking care of runaway slaves. In 1865 the Freedmen's Bureau took over Freedman's Village, which at that time was basically a refugee camp, and turned it into a real village with schools, training centers, hospitals, churches, and farms.

Sojourner Truth's Role. Famous African Americans like Sojourner Truth came to Freedman's Village to advise the now-free slaves and to help them get jobs in the Washington, D.C., area and up North. Truth was a mainstay at Freedman's Village and Washington, D.C.'s, newest hospital, Freedman's Hospital.

More than just a preacher, Sojourner Truth also was a protector for the people of the Freedman's Village. Slave owners from Maryland had taken to raiding the Freedman's Village for black children to work for them, and if the children's parents complained, they were thrown in jail. But Truth went through the village telling parents that they didn't have to stand for such treatment, because they had rights as well.

Some of the whites in the area were upset that an African-American woman was telling freed slaves about their rights, and they threatened to throw Sojourner Truth in prison. She wasn't intimidated in the slightest, however. If they tried to silence her, Sojourner Truth warned them that she would "make this nation rock like a cradle." She was left alone.

Truth had powerful friends, and she knew it. While living and working at Freedman's Village, she was likely the first African-American woman to be received at the White House as a guest of the president in his office.

Her work at Freedman's Village didn't mark the only time Sojourner Truth would challenge the white power structure of the District of Columbia. She wasn't

Sojourner Truth

One of the most famous African-American women of her time, Sojourner Truth was best known for the book about her life, *The Narrative of Sojourner Truth: A Northern Slave,* which was written by Olive Gilbert and published by William Lloyd Garrison in 1850.

MORE FACTS

Born Isabella Baumfree in New York State in the late 1790s, Truth was the daughter of slaves and therefore began her life as a slave. In 1826 she escaped with one of her four children, saying later, "I did not run off, for I thought that wicked, but I walked off, believing that to be all right."

A devout Christian, Baumfree changed her name to Sojourner Truth in 1843 and became a traveling preacher and abolitionist, preaching about the evils of slavery to anyone who would listen. Her most famous speech was "Ain't I a Woman?" which was given at the Women's Rights Convention in Akron, Ohio, on May 28, 1851. Truth told the crowd that women deserve the same rights as men because they are equal in capability to men. The speech is remembered to this day.

afraid to take her causes to the courts when she knew she was right. She was the first African-American woman to win a lawsuit against a white man. When a slave owner illegally sold her son Peter to Alabama, she took the slave owner to court. She won the case, and her son was returned. But she didn't stop there. Sojourner Truth also won a slander case and a $125 judgment against a newspaper that called her a "witch" who poisoned a leader of a religious group.

Sojourner Truth and Washington Public Transportation. When Sojourner Truth moved to Freedman's Village, she needed to ride Washington's streetcars to get to her job at the Freedman's Hospital in the city. However, the District had a strict policy of segregation on its public transportation, and African Americans had to sit in special sections in the streetcars. Truth decided that she would not stand for this, and long before Rosa Parks, she decided to conduct "ride-ins" on the streetcars to protest. An addition to a later printing of her *Narrative,* called the *Book of Life,* describes one of the incidents:

Sojourner signaled the car, but neither conductor nor driver noticed her. Soon another followed, and she raised her hand again, but they also turned away. She then gave three tremendous yelps, "I want to ride! I want to ride!! I want to ride!!! Consternation seized the passing crowd—people, carriages, go-carts of every description stood still. The car was effectually blocked up, and before it could move on, Sojourner had jumped aboard. Then there arose a great shout from the crowd, "Ha! ha! ha!! She has beaten him." The angry conductor told her to go forward where the horses were, or he would put her out. Quietly seating herself, she informed him that she was a passenger. "Go forward where the horses are, or I will throw you out," said he in a menacing voice. She told him that she was neither a Marylander nor a Virginian to fear his threats; but was from the Empire State of New York, and knew the laws as well as he did.

Several soldiers were in the car, and when other passengers came in, they related the circumstance and said, "You ought to have heard that old woman talk to the conductor." Sojourner rode farther than she needed to go; for a ride was so rare a privilege that she determined to make the most of it. She left the car feeling very happy, and said, "Bless God! I have had a ride."

On another occasion, Truth had been walking with a white friend when they decided to take a streetcar together. This time, a conductor put his hand on her to force her off the streetcar, and the situation exploded. In the *Book of Life*, Truth described the events that transpired:

As Mrs. Haviland signaled the car, I stepped one side as if to continue my walk and when it stopped I ran and jumped aboard. The conductor pushed me back, saying, "Get out of the way and let this lady come in." "Whoop!" said I, "I am a lady too." We went with no further opposition till we were obliged to change cars. A man coming out as we were going into the next car, asked the conductor if "niggers were allowed to ride." The conductor grabbed me by the shoulder and jerking me around, ordered me to get out. I told him I would not. Mrs. Haviland took hold of my other arm and said, "Don't put her out." The conductor asked if I belonged to her. "No," replied Mrs. Haviland, "She belongs to humanity." "Then take her and go," said he, and giving me another push slammed me against the door. I told him I would let him know whether he could shove me about like a dog, and said to Mrs. Haviland, "Take the number of this car."

Truth found out during a hospital visit that she had a case to take this man to court for assault and battery. With the assistance of a lawyer from the Freedmen's Bureau, she won. Her lawsuit not only got the streetcar conductor fired, it also became one of the catalysts that forced the District to desegregate its street-cars. "It created a great sensation, and before the trial was ended, the inside of the cars looked like pepper and salt," Truth said in the *Book of Life*.

Self-Improvement. Sojourner Truth brought hope to the Freedman's Village, but residents also helped themselves by educating and taking care of their own. They turned what started out as a refugee camp into a real home, building houses and schools. Wooden two-story duplex houses were built, housing multiple families. There were also homes set up for the old and infirm, who could not care for themselves.

A school was also constructed, enrolling as many as nine hundred students at one time. An observer's description of the facility was recorded in *Addresses and Ceremonies at the New Year's Festival to the Freedmen, on Arlington Heights*, a pamphlet found in the *Pamphlets from the Daniel A. P. Murray Collection, 1818–1907* at the Library of Congress:

> A school had been previously organized by Mr. Sperry, of the American Tract Society, under a majestic oak, near to a fine spring of pure water. Under the earnest and faithful labors of the superintendent and others, hundreds of children and adults received the rudiments of education, and were instructed in religious knowledge.

The school also taught them trades so that they could become blacksmiths, wheelwrights, carpenters, shoemakers, or tailors. The students then gave back to the village, making clothes and shoes for the villagers and chairs and desks for the school.

In 1866 Abbott Hospital was established in Freedman's Village. It contained fifty beds and a staff of fourteen. Meanwhile, the American Tract Society of Washington set up a church. The *Addresses and Ceremonies* pamphlet provides a description of the church, quoting a white woman who went to a festival in Freedman's Village:

> The chapel, a large, unplastered building, whose adornment had been left entirely to the colored people, bore witness to an unusual simplicity of taste. Its sides were hung with evergreen. The only motto (that placed above the speaker's stand) was the name of Lincoln, while across the room was suspended the flag!—the flag which at last means all to the black man that it does to the white, and which to-day means more to us all than it ever could before.

The woman went on to describe how lovely the views of the capital were from Freedman's Village:

> The beautiful views from Freedman's Village may be why it doesn't exist anymore. After the Civil War ended, the desire to help freed slaves dwindled in the federal government and the Lee family wanted Arlington House and the estate back.

The Demise. In December 1882 the Lee family won a lawsuit they brought to the U.S. Supreme Court regarding Arlington House. The five-four ruling stated that Arlington House had been confiscated without due process. The next year Congress purchased the property from the Lees for $150,000.

Arlington House officially became government property and Freedman's Village was finished. On December 7, 1887, the people in the village were given ninety days to leave. They received $75,000 to split amongst themselves as compensation for the work they did to make their homes livable. Then they were thrown off the land. Today nothing is left of Freedman's Village. However, that doesn't mean that there is no record of the African Americans who used to live at

Graves of freed men, women, and children in Section 27 of Arlington National Cemetery

the site that became Arlington National Cemetery. The federal government removed the buildings but left behind the grave sites of those who died there.

In Section 27 of the cemetery, the part of Arlington National Cemetery closest to the Iwo Jima Memorial, there are more than 3,800 grave markers with inscriptions bearing the words "civilian" and "citizen." These are the graves of the former residents of Freedman's Village, who are laid to rest near the land they used to call their own.

Interred with the residents of Freedman's Village in Section 27 (and also Section 23) are about 1,500 United States Colored Troops, the African Americans who fought with the Union Army despite being forced to work in segregated units. Their tombstones bear a Civil War Shield and the letters U.S.C.T. carved on the front. The troops are buried in these two sections because Arlington National Cemetery was segregated for more than eighty years, and African-American war dead were buried separately from their white counterparts.

Mount Vernon

George Washington's Home

Mount Vernon is a shrine to the first president of the United States, George Washington. Washington inherited Mount Vernon in 1761, and by the time he died in 1799, he had purchased additional land and increased his holdings from two thousand to nearly eight thousand acres. From Mount Vernon, Washington raised his family, accepted his first military command, introduced the use of mules to America, and discovered his destiny as the general of the American army and first president of the United States.

Mount Vernon was saved from disrepair and possible destruction in 1858 when the Mount Vernon Ladies' Association of the Union obtained the land from Washington's great-grandnephew, John A. Washington Jr., and restored the buildings and grounds. Today Mount Vernon appears as it did when Washington died in 1799—a majestic estate where a gentleman farmer could relax and reap the benefits of land ownership and free labor (because in addition to being the father of our country, Washington was also a major slaveholder, keeping hundreds of African Americans at his Mount Vernon plantation).

George Washington's Slaves. Records show that when Washington first began farming Mount Vernon, he owned about thirty-six slaves. He obtained even more through inheritance, marriage, and slave breeding, and by the time Washington died, there were 316 slaves living at Mount Vernon.

Mount Vernon as we see it today would not have been as successful or as impressive without the slave labor under Washington. Slaves provided most of the skilled and unskilled labor that was used to run the plantation. In fact, part of the reason we know what Mount Vernon looked like when George Washington died is because of a slave named West Ford. West Ford (1784–1863), based upon his personal recollection, provided the Mount Vernon Ladies' Association with intimate details about Mount Vernon's interior decoration when the association purchased it and decided to restore it to historical accuracy.

Ford worked as a manager at Mount Vernon after Washington's death, and he is one of the African Americans believed to be buried at Mount Vernon. After being freed from slavery, Ford worked as a free man for several generations of Washington's descendants who inherited Mount Vernon following the death of Martha Washington in 1802. He also became a prominent member of the African-American community and founded a free African-American settlement near Mount Vernon called Gum Springs.

Ford is better known these days as possibly being the child of George Washington and a slave woman. Ford was born into slavery around 1784 at the plantation of Washington's brother, John Augustine Washington, in Westmoreland County, Virginia. Ford's mother was a slave named Venus; his father's identity has never been firmly established. However, Ford's family has an oral tradition indicating that Venus told George Washington's sister-in-law that George Washington was her child's father. There is no documentary evidence to support that claim or to disprove it. What is known, however, is that Washington's sister-in-law ordered West Ford to be educated and freed when he reached the age of twenty-one.

After Martha Washington's death, Ford moved to the Mount Vernon plantation, where he was treated as a privileged servant. Ford even became the first tomb guard for George Washington's grave site, a title he passed down to three generations of Fords.

Another Washington, Bushrod Washington, willed 160 acres of land adjacent to Mount Vernon to West Ford, who sold the land and bought 214 acres adjacent to it. This area is known today as the African-American community of Gum Springs, Virginia.

An ailing West Ford returned to Mount Vernon at the end of his life. The Mount Vernon Ladies' Association cared for Ford until his death on July 20, 1863. Ford was then buried on Mount Vernon, either in the slave cemetery or in Washington's tomb, a spot that he guarded for years.

If the story of his parentage is true, Ford would not be the only African-American member of Washington's family. Martha Washington's younger illegitimate half-sister was a slave named Ann Dandridge Costin, who was one-quarter African, one-quarter Cherokee Indian, and half white. In his 2003 book *An Imperfect God: George Washington, His Slaves, and the Creation of America,* historian Henry Wiencek says Martha Washington owned Ann, who in turn had a child by Martha's son (Ann's nephew), John Parke "Jack" Custis.

The Mount Vernon Slave Memorial

The slave cemetery is one of the major African-American tourist sites at Mount Vernon, as it is the final resting site of about three hundred of Washington's slaves.

The original Mount Vernon Slave Memorial

The Freeing of Washington's Slaves

Washington arranged for all of the slaves he personally owned to be freed after he and his wife Martha died. His will was specific: "Upon the decease of my wife, it is my Will and desire that all the Slaves which I hold in my own right shall receive their freedom . . . And I do hereby expressly forbid the Sale, or transportation out of said Commonwealth, of any Slave I may die possessed of, under any pretence whatsoever."

Martha Washington did not wait until her death to free the slaves, however. On January 1, 1801, she legally freed Washington's slaves. This does not mean that all of the slaves at Mount Vernon were able to obtain their freedom, however. Only 123 slaves at Mount Vernon belonged to George Washington. Another forty belonged to Washington's neighbors and were only rented out to Mount Vernon. They had to be returned to their owners.

There were also other slaves at Mount Vernon who were not able to gain their freedom. They were "dower" slaves, meaning they belonged to the estate of Martha Washington's first husband. By law, the dower slaves legally belonged to Daniel Custis's heirs, who took possession of them after Martha Washington died in 1802.

In 1929 the Mount Vernon Ladies' Association marked the site with a flat tablet of Georgian marble. The tablet reads: In memory of the many faithful colored Servants of the Washington family buried at Mount Vernon from 1760 to 1860 / their unidentified graves surround this spot / 1929.

In 1983 a woman named Judith Saunders-Burton helped lead efforts to improve the slave cemetery. Howard University architecture students designed the current memorial, which now features two park benches and a gravel path leading to a circular plaza. The plaza contains a granite column in its center atop three concentric circles inscribed with the words faith, hope and love. A terrace around the shaft bears the following inscription: In Memory of the Afro Americans Who Served as Slaves At Mount Vernon This Monument Marking Their Burial Ground Dedicated September 21, 1983 Mount Vernon Ladies' Association.

Slave Quarters at Mount Vernon

The Mount Vernon Slave Memorial is not the only record of slave life at George Washington's plantation. Newer brick slave quarters were added to Washington's greenhouse in 1793, and that building still exists at Mount Vernon. The four rectangular rooms provided housing for most of the Mansion House Farm slaves.

Washington had divided Mount Vernon into five farms, putting about a third of Mount Vernon's slave population at the Mansion House Farm. Many of those slaves lived in the greenhouse slave quarters. Although they were still slave quarters, these buildings were better than the dirty log cabins other Mount Vernon slaves were forced to sleep in. Each building was constructed of brick and featured a fireplace and glazed windows.

The current Mount Vernon Slave Memorial is believed to be the only such tribute at a plantation in the United States to the African Americans who were enslaved there.

These facilities were crowded, however. One family at the Mansion House Farm consisted of a man named Isaac, a carpenter; his wife Kitty, a dairy maid; and their nine daughters. Four spaces of similar size in the Greenhouse Quarters housed other large families.

Health problems were often made worse by close quarters. Slaves suffered from fleas, intestinal parasites, and body mites. Children were especially susceptible to respiratory and intestinal problems and frequently suffered accidents.

During a February 15, 2004, interview on the CBS show *Early Morning,* historian Henry Wiencek said that Washington was trying to hide the slave quarters because he was beginning to oppose slavery. "You don't know that those are the slave quarters. There are no doors, there are very small windows. He made it invisible," Wiencek said.

Alexandria

Alexandria Black History Museum

The Alexandria Black History Museum holds a unique place in African-American history: It exists because of what is believed to be the very first civil rights sit-in in American history.

The most famous sit-in was at the Woolworth's in Greensboro, North Carolina. On February 1, 1960, four African-American students from North Carolina A&T State University decided that discrimination at food establishments in North Carolina was wrong. They sat down at a lunch counter at Woolworth's and politely asked for service. When they were refused service and were asked to leave, they remained in their seats until the building closed that evening.

The students' courageous action helped ignite peaceful sit-ins around the country, which helped bring attention to the unlawful segregation in many facilities in the South and other areas of the country. Following the lead of the North Carolina college students, nonviolent sit-ins spread across the country and helped launch the modern civil rights movement. The incident was so important that the Woolworth's lunch counter has been preserved by the Smithsonian Institution.

The Woolworth's sit-in was not the first successful civil rights sit-in, however. Most people don't know that the sit-in had already been successfully used to effect change in Alexandria, Virginia.

The building now being used for the Alexandria Black History Museum was originally the Robert Robinson Library, one of the few public libraries for African Americans in the United States in the 1940s. The city of Alexandria opened this facility after five young African Americans—William Evans, Otto L. Tucker, Edward Gaddis, Morris Murray, and Clarence Strange—walked into the city's segregated Queen Street Library in 1939 and insisted that they be allowed to check out and read the books inside. The assistant librarian asked the five men to leave, saying the library was for whites only. Instead of leaving, the men went to the stacks, picked out books, and sat down at tables to read.

Soon, the head librarian, the chief of police, and several officers showed up at the library. When they arrived, they found about three hundred spectators and the news media. Entering the library, the police officers arrested the five men for refusing to leave. The local newspaper, *The Alexandria Gazette,* reported the incident in its August 21, 1939 issue:

> Five colored youths were arrested on a charge of disorderly conduct today on the complaint of Policeman John F. Kelley after they entered the Alexandria Library, withdrew books from the shelves and sat down at a table to read, despite the fact that they were asked to leave by Librarian Miss Catherine Scoggin.

The five men had legal help waiting, however. The sit-in had been organized by civil rights lawyer Samuel Wilbert Tucker, who also had been denied a library card at the Queen Street Library earlier that year. He decided that he had had enough of segregation. One of his mentors from Howard University had just returned from India, where tales of Gandhi's nonviolent resistance had inspired Tucker. Training five men, including his brother Otto L. Tucker, Tucker waited for his chance, and it came as the five men were arrested by Alexandria police for their sit-in at the library.

The five young men were charged with disorderly conduct, but Tucker had his opportunity for a public hearing. When the case made it to court, Tucker won. The judge found no regulation limiting the library's use to whites; it was open to all Alexandria residents and taxpayers since there was no library for African Americans. However, instead of integrating the library, the city moved quickly to build a "colored library" in the Parker-Gray neighborhood. The library, named for the Reverend Robert H. Robinson, opened April 23, 1940.

From 1940 to 1960, most African Americans in Alexandria used the Robert Robinson Library to read and study. After the 1960s the city library system was desegregated and the building was used for community service programs. The Alexandria Black History Museum opened in the space in 1989.

The museum has two galleries: the Parker-Gray Gallery for temporary exhibits, and the Robert Robinson Library, which holds the museum's permanent exhibition gallery and contains an exhibition on African-American business in Alexandria. *Alexandria Black History Museum; 638 North Alfred Street, Alexandria, VA; 703-838-4356.*

Alexandria African American Heritage Park

The Alexandria African American Heritage Park is also part of the Alexandria Black History Museum complex. Dedicated in 1995, the nine-acre park was the original site of an 1885 African American Baptist Cemetery, one of Alexandria's earliest African-American graveyards. Six of the twenty-one original headstones are still intact and in their original location. There is also a sculpture group, a burial mound, and three twelve- to fifteen-foot bronze trees bearing the names of Alexandria's African-American leaders, doctors, lawyers, printers, schools, churches, and one event: the Alexandria library sit-in of 1939.

Petersburg

Petersburg National Battlefield Park

Very few African Americans visit Civil War historical sites like battlefields and cemeteries, and why should they? For decades the Civil War has been portrayed as a battle between white Union and Confederate soldiers, with a lot of slaves but only a few black soldiers looking on from the side. This was not the reality, however.

Black troops took part in almost 450 engagements between 1862 and 1865, with black men making up about one in every eight Union soldiers by the time the War between the States ended. These men were risking even more than the Union's white soldiers, who had a hope of being held in a prisoner-of-war camp if they lost a battle to the Confederates. Black soldiers could only hope for a quick death, because the rebels routinely killed any black who raised a weapon against them, whether they surrendered or not.

The Petersburg National Battlefield Park is one of the few—if not the only—national Civil War battlefield site that has erected memorials and markers to the black soldiers who fought and died on its fields.

Petersburg was the location of the longest siege in American history, with Gen. Ulysses S. Grant attempting to cut off Gen. Robert E. Lee's supply lines into Petersburg and Richmond, the capital of the Confederacy. On April 2, 1865, nine and a half months after the siege began, Lee evacuated Petersburg. His surrender at Appomattox Court House was just a week away.

Blacks were present on both sides of the battle from the beginning. Petersburg is thought to have had the largest number of free blacks of any Southern city. Many stayed and even worked for the Confederacy after the Civil War began. They served in various positions, working as barbers, blacksmiths, boatmen, draymen, livery-stable keepers, and caterers.

Petersburg was important because it was a major supply center for the newly formed Confederacy and its nearby capital in Richmond. Five railroad tracks and numerous important roads ran in and out of the city, and quite a few blacks worked for the railroad companies supplying the Confederate army.

Because of Petersburg's importance and its location twenty-five miles south of Richmond, defending the city became vital to the burgeoning Confederacy. As a result, in 1862–1863, Capt. Charles Dimmock of the Confederacy decided that the city needed a ten-mile-long defensive line of trenches and batteries in case the Union Army decided to attack. These defenses were built by Confederate soldiers, free blacks (who were paid for their efforts), and slaves, who of course never received a penny for their work.

Once the siege of Petersburg began, blacks continued to work for the Confederacy. The rebels' impending defeat even prompted the South to consider arming blacks to fight for their side. A notice in the April 1, 1865, *Petersburg Daily Express* called for black recruits: "To the slaves is offered freedom and undisturbed residences at their old homes in the Confederacy after the war. Not freedom of sufferance, but honorable and selfwon by the gallantry and devotion which grateful countrymen will never cease to remember and reward."

The war ended before anyone could take the Confederacy up on its offer. When the Confederate Army surrendered at Appomattox, a total of thirty-six blacks were with them. All were listed as cooks, teamsters, musicians, and other civilian titles.

On the Union side, the nation's greatest concentration of United States Colored Troops (USCT) was located at Petersburg. Nearly 8,000 of the more than 185,000 black soldiers enlisted in the Civil War were involved in the siege of Petersburg. The black soldiers were supposed to be the principal part of what should have been the Union's greatest victory. Instead, they were part of what general and future president Ulysses Grant ended up calling "the saddest affair [he had] witnessed in this war."

To penetrate the defenses around Petersburg, Union Lt. Col. Henry Pleasants came up with a plan. Instead of charging directly at the Confederates, Pleasants suggested that he and the men of the 48th Pennsylvania Infantry—many of whom were miners—dig a tunnel underneath the enemy's fortifications and blow them up with four tons of explosive powder. If successful, this would not only kill all the defenders in the area, it would also open a hole in the Confederate defenses and cause the fall of Petersburg.

While the miners were digging the tunnel, the nine USCT regiments that made up the 4th Division of IX Corps trained to exploit the Confederates' confusion and charge through the gap in the rebel lines. Finally, when the day of the attack came, the 4th Division was ready and the 48th Pennsylvania was ready. But before the tunnel was detonated, the Union leaders decided to make a last-second change: They pulled the 4th Division out of the attack plan and inserted new troops—the white 1st, 2nd, and 3rd Divisions.

The explosion killed an entire Confederate regiment, but the untrained white Union troops rushed forward into the crater and discovered that they couldn't negotiate their way out the other side. The Confederate soldiers that were still alive soon regrouped and found the Union soldiers floundering about in the crater in front of them. The U.S soldiers were easy targets for the Confederates, and the slaughter began.

Even though Union leaders could tell that this battle was a bloody failure, they sent the 4th Division into the crater anyway, where they were slaughtered along with their white comrades. "The colored troops made a very spirited attack, and behaved remarkably well while coming up," said Bevert Major Gen. O. B. Wilcox during the congressional investigation. "But the place they came into was a place where we could hardly hope for any success."

Officials reported that more than 1,300 members of the United States Colored Troops were lost in that battle, although some people put the true number at more than 2,000—about half of all Union casualties during the Battle of the Crater.

The Union attack failed and the siege of Petersburg went on. In the aftermath, even Grant himself said that if they had sent the black troops in first, the battle could have been won. "General Burnside wanted to put his colored division in front, and I believe if he had done so it would have been a success," Grant told Congress.

The most honored black troops in the Civil War were part of the Army of the James, which was made up of the troops that had been stationed around Petersburg. They played a key role in the Battle of New Market Heights, the North's most successful effort to break Gen. Robert E. Lee's defensive lines.

The black division of the XVIII Corps was sent to take the earthworks along the New Market Road below New Market Heights, but more than 2,000 Confederate soldiers were waiting behind the earthworks. After being pinned down by Confederate artillery fire for about thirty minutes, the black soldiers charged the earthworks and rushed up the slopes of the heights. The first to enter were 1st Sgt. Edward Ratcliff, Sgt. James Harris, and Pvt. William Barnes, all of the 38th Regiment, United States Colored Troops. During the hourlong engagement the division suffered tremendous casualties. Of the 3,000 black troops engaged, more than 1,300 were killed, wounded, or missing in fewer than two hours of fighting.

By the time the Petersburg campaign ended, African-American soldiers had participated in six major engagements; and fourteen of the African-Americans who were awarded the Medal of Honor during the Civil War received the medal because of their actions at New Market Heights. In the middle of the Petersburg National Battlefield Park, there is a monument to the United States Colored Troops who fought in this area. The monument was erected near where the African-American soldiers captured Confederate Battery 9 of the Dimmock Line. The monument reads: In memory of the valorous service of regiments and companies of the U.S. Colored Troops, Army of the James and Army of the Potomac. Siege of Petersburg 1864–1865.

Manassas

Manassas National Battlefield Park

The Manassas National Battlefield Park is the location of two of the most important battles of the Civil War, the Battles of Bull Run. With its victory at Manassas in 1861, the Confederacy showed that the Civil War would not be an overnight war; and a famous Southern officer, Thomas Jackson, gained his famous nickname: "Stonewall" Jackson. The next year, the Union again was crushed at Manassas under the weight of twenty-eight thousand Confederates, the largest simultaneous mass assault of the war.

Unlike Petersburg, the battles at Manassas came too early in the Civil War for black soldiers to participate. However, that doesn't mean there's no significant African-American history at Manassas National Battlefield Park. Inside the park, archeologists are working on the Robinson House, a site that may help people understand how free and enslaved blacks lived before and during the Civil War.

Home of a Free African-American Family: The Robinsons. The Robinson House site is the former home of a free African-American family who had the unfortunate luck of living right in the middle of what would become a major Civil War battlefield. A historical marker referencing this site can be found on Highway 29 near the national park.

Born in 1799, James "Gentleman" Robinson earned the $484.94 needed to purchase 170 acres of land near Bull Run by working in a tavern. In 1842 he built a small log cabin, which was enlarged and renovated several times over the years. Robinson married Susan Gaskins, who was enslaved by John Lee, a Manassas resident. Robinson and his wife had six children, all born into slavery, but Robinson bought two of his sons' freedom, and three others were released on Lee's death in 1847 or after the Civil War ended.

On July 21, 1861, the first Battle of Manassas erupted around the Robinson house. Robinson was able to get his family out to safety, but he ended up trapped in the middle of the battle himself. Robinson family tradition holds that after getting some valuables, Robinson took refuge under the turnpike bridge at Young's Branch as hundreds of Confederates streamed through his yard, retreating from the Union attack. When Robinson made it back to his house, there

were thirteen Confederate soldiers lying dead in his front yard. The house, however, survived the battle virtually intact.

The Robinsons returned to their home only to have the second Battle of
Manassas erupt on their property. This time, the Robinson house wasn't as lucky.
Union troops took over the house, sacking it and the nearby fields, eventually
using the Robinson house as their field hospital.

On September 11, 1862, a *Charleston Daily Courier* newspaper report by
Felix Gregory de Fontaine described the conditions inside the house under its
Union occupation:

> The Robinson House is used as a Yankee hospital. In a visit there this
> morning, I found 100 of them packed in the rooms as thick as sardines. The
> wounds of the majority were undressed, the blood had dried upon their per-
> sons and garments, and altogether there the most horrible set of beings it has
> been my lot to encounter.

After the war Robinson convinced Congress to compensate him for the use
of his house and lands. On March 3, 1873, Congress awarded Robinson $1,249
for his losses through a private act.

The Robinsons persevered through the struggles over their land, with patriarch Robinson leaving behind 1,500 acres when he died of heart disease in 1875.
The Robinsons continued to live on their land and in their house, even making
structural additions to it, through 1924, when they sold the property to the
Manassas Battlefield Park.

The Robinson house stood until 1993, when arsonists burned part of the
structure. The Robinson family site is now of great interest to archeologists
because it is one of the few home sites of free eighteenth- and nineteenth-
century black families still left to be studied. Archeologists have found thousands
of artifacts, including papers written with the signature of Jim "Gentleman"
Robinson. The foundation of the house is still visible in the park, with three
interpretive outdoor signs explaining the history of the site.

The Robinsons are also referenced inside the museum, where there is an
exhibit dedicated to the Robinson family, including an etched drawing of the
house as it appeared in the mid-nineteenth century and artifacts related to the
house's use as a hospital during the Civil War.

CHAPTER SEVEN

On the VERGE OF A TRUE BLACK RENAISSANCE

As of this writing, the nation's capital is on the verge of a true black renaissance, considering the African-American monuments, memorials, and museums that are planned or already under construction in Washington, D.C., and the surrounding areas.

The importance of recognizing African-American contributions to the founding and prosperity of America has been approved by no less than the United States Congress itself, which has authorized three more memorials to be built on the National Mall: the Smithsonian Museum of African American History and Culture; the Martin Luther King Jr. National Memorial; and the Black Patriots Revolutionary War Monument, which supporters now are trying to upgrade to the Liberty National Monument.

Some have complained that with so many different projects honoring African Americans, support from the public will be diluted to the point where all of the projects will suffer and struggle to be completed on time. Douglass Wilder, who became the first African-American governor in America's history when he won the top seat in Virginia (a former slaveholding state and capital of the Confederacy) disputes this idea. There are thousands of other art galleries and history museums around the country—with more being opened every day—and they all find ways to coexist and not compete, said Wilder, who is now mayor of Richmond, Virginia, the former capital of the Confederacy. The African-American-themed projects will have to do the same thing. "You can't have too many. There is enough money to go around," said Wilder (who is also the founder of the forthcoming National Slavery Museum in

Fredericksburg, Virginia) during a Black History Month speech at the National Press Club in February 2006.

All of the following monuments, memorials, and museums are still raising money to aid their completion, and all opening dates are subject to change. If you wish to volunteer your time or donate, mailing addresses, Web sites, and telephone numbers are provided where available. To find out more about what you'll be able to see in Washington, D.C., and the surrounding areas in the future, read on.

Rosa Parks Statue in the United States Capitol

Unveiling date: Late 2007–Early 2008
Location: Washington, D.C., the National Statuary Hall inside the U.S. Capitol

Rosa Parks is known as the mother of the civil rights movement because of her refusal to give up her seat on a Montgomery, Alabama, public bus to a white man. Her decision led to the famous Montgomery bus boycott and the rising national prominence of a young black minister named Martin Luther King Jr.

Parks, who for decades symbolized the beginning of the civil rights movement, died in October 2005. Parks was the first woman (as well as the second nongovernmental official and only the second African American) in America's history to lie in honor in the U.S. Capitol's Rotunda—quite an honor for a former seamstress.

Photograph of Rosa Parks with Dr. King, around 1955

Days after her funeral, Congress passed legislation to place a statue of Parks inside the Capitol; President George W. Bush signed this legislation on December 1, 2005, the fortieth anniversary of Parks's act of civil disobedience. The law requires that the Rosa Parks statue be placed inside the National Statuary Hall—the former U.S. House of Representatives chamber that already houses more than thirty statues of prominent people from American history—before the end of 2007. A design competition to pick the sculptor of the Rosa Parks statue will be held later in the year by the Architect of the Capitol.

The United States National Slavery Museum

Opening date: 2008
Location: Fredericksburg, Virginia
www.usnsm.org
540-548-8818
Donations can be sent to:
The United States National Slavery Museum
1320 Central Park Boulevard, Suite 251
Fredericksburg, VA 22401

The United States National Slavery Museum in Fredericksburg, Virginia—scheduled to open in late 2008—will be the first museum in the United States dedicated to understanding and studying the impact of slavery on America's culture, economy, and society.

Located halfway between Washington, D.C., and Richmond, Virginia—the capitals of the North and the South, respectively, during the Civil War—it will also serve as a memorial to the tens of millions of African men, women, and children who were taken from their homelands in the seventeenth and eighteenth centuries and brought to this country as slaves.

Rising from thirty-eight acres nestled on the banks of the Rappahannock River, the museum will feature a full-scale replica of the ship *Dos Amigos,* a slaving schooner active in the first half of the nineteenth century. Inside, visitors will be able to experience firsthand the cramped quarters and squalid conditions that millions of slaves endured for months at a time as they were taken across the Atlantic.

The ship will be the museum's signature feature, with the building's ceiling extending into the air to allow for the full height of the *Dos Amigos* and creating a distinctive skyline for people traveling southbound on nearby Interstate 95. When completed, the *Dos Amigos* will be the largest indoor replica ship in the United States.

Other planned exhibits include:

— The United States National Slavery Museum Library, featuring oral histories, maps, rare editions, film, and video, all telling the individual and collective stories of a people searching for freedom.

— Truth & Reflection, a gallery encouraging onlookers to examine slavery through the broad spectrum of world history and its racial connotation in American society.

— Genius and Ingenuity: The Integral Role of Slaves in America, an examination of the contributions slaves made to American society despite the great tribulations they faced.

Also inside the museum will be 100,000 square feet of permanent and temporary exhibit space, classrooms, lecture halls, a 450-seat theater, virtual-reality exhibits, and a library with a capacity of 250,000 books relating to the institution of slavery in the United States and its aftermath in our society. Outside the museum, along the banks of the Rappahannock River, will be working cotton and tobacco fields, the main cash crops that slaves were brought to America to work.

The museum was designed by C. C. Pei of Pei Partnership Architects of New York City, whose other works include the Grand Louvre in Paris, the Museum of Fine Arts West Wing in Boston, and the modernization of Mt. Sinai Medical Center in New York City.

"The U.S. National Slavery Museum will paint a complete picture of what slavery meant and means to America, so visitors can commemorate, understand, and most importantly, overcome its painful legacy," said Douglass Wilder, the museum's founder, the first African-American governor in Virginia.

The Smithsonian Institution National Museum of African American History and Culture

Opening date: 2015
Location: Washington, D.C., 14th Street NW and Constitution Avenue
www.nmaahc.si.edu
Donations can be sent to:
National Museum of African American History and Culture
Smithsonian Institution
Department 0544
Washington, D.C. 20073-0544

After almost a century of dreaming, battling, and planning, the soon-to-be-constructed Smithsonian Institution National Museum of African American History and Culture is finally on its way to becoming a reality in the nation's capital. The National Museum of African American History and Culture, to be located in a prominent spot on the National Mall, will become the first and only national museum in North America devoted solely to documenting and displaying relics of African-American life, art, history, and culture.

While efforts to create such a museum have been under way since 1916, the dream finally became a reality on December 19, 2003, when President George W. Bush signed legislation that officially designated the museum as part of the Smithsonian Institution and required it to be placed somewhere near the National Mall in Washington. The federal government will pay for half of the cost of constructing the museum, while the rest will be collected through private donations.

In early 2006, the museum's board decided to locate the museum near the center of the National Mall bordering the Washington Monument, the Ellipse, the Department of Commerce, and the Smithsonian National Museum of American History. The five-acre site (which is currently empty) is part of the original Mall and has been controlled by the U.S. government since 1791. Construction on the museum will begin in the next few years, and directors hope to open its doors before 2010.

Unlike most of the Smithsonian's museums, the National Museum of African American History and Culture does not have a preexisting collection of artifacts to build around. After construction begins, directors plan to scour the country to

Future site of the Smithsonian Institution National Museum of African American History and Culture PHOTO COURTESY OF THE SMITHSONIAN INSTITUTION

find exhibits for the museum to help fulfill its mission: "the collection, study, and establishment of programs relating to African-American life, art, history, and culture that encompass the period of slavery, the era of Reconstruction, the Harlem renaissance, the civil rights movement and other periods of the African American diaspora." NMAAHC director Lonnie Bunch said in a 2005 interview on National Public Radio that he's looking for "artifacts that will tell the story of Black life, whether it's things as diverse as movie posters or maybe the lunch counters from the Greensboro sit-in, but you'll see things that'll move you."

The building will have enough room to fit almost anything inside. Builders estimate that the museum will take up at least 350,000 square feet and stand about 75 feet high, about the same height as the nearby National Museum of American History.

The national scope of the museum will help differentiate it from its two sister Smithsonian museums: The Smithsonian Institution's Anacostia Museum and Center for African American History and Culture and the Smithsonian Institution's National Museum of African Art. The Anacostia Museum began as a neighborhood museum in 1967 and expanded to help fulfill its mission over the years to include African-American materials from around the country. Meanwhile, the National Museum of African Art, also located on the National Mall, is devoted solely to the art of the continent of Africa. The National Museum of African American History and Culture, however, will be dedicated to a national "collection, preservation, research, and exhibition of African-American historical and cultural material reflecting the breadth and depth of the experiences of individuals of African descent living in the United States," according to the congressional legislation establishing the museum.

The Martin Luther King Jr. National Memorial

Opening date: 2008
Location: Washington, D.C., on the Tidal Basin adjacent to the Franklin Delano Roosevelt Memorial and near the Lincoln Memorial
www.buildthedream.org
Donations can be sent to:
Washington D.C. Martin Luther King Jr. National Memorial Project Foundation, Inc.
Department 211
Washington, D.C. 20055

Martin Luther King Jr. will become the first African-American man and the first nonpresident to be honored with a memorial on the National Mall when a national monument dedicated in his name opens in 2008, marking the fortieth anniversary of his assassination.

The Martin Luther King Jr. National Memorial will be located on a four-acre plot on the Tidal Basin adjacent to the Franklin Delano Roosevelt Memorial and midway between the Jefferson Memorial and the Lincoln Memorial. The centerpiece of the monument will be a granite block called *The Stone of Hope,* which will feature a thirty-foot likeness of Martin Luther King Jr. looking out over the Tidal Basin toward the Jefferson Memorial. In King's hands will be a pencil pointing back toward the stone's inscription, called *The Promissory Note,* part of King's famous 1968 "I Have a Dream" speech at the Lincoln Memorial.

Surrounding the centerpiece will be a curving stone wall carrying excerpts of King's sermons, more quotes from the "I Have a Dream" speech, gurgling streams that coalesce into a flowing water wall, and random groupings of Washington's famous cherry trees as well as oaks, pines, and magnolia trees. An original design had one source of the water being "martyrs' wells," which are individually crafted niches adjacent to the main path. Combined, the water, stone, and trees will symbolize justice, democracy, and hope, three themes interwoven in the life of America's greatest civil rights leader. Interspersed throughout the monument will be more King quotations, with room left over to honor other civil rights pioneers like Coretta Scott King, Fannie Lou Hamer, or Rosa Parks.

Supporters broke ground on the memorial in November 2006, placing a plaque at the spot where the memorial will be located. The federal government has pledged $10 million toward the construction of the Martin Luther King Jr. National Memorial, with the rest of the $100 million cost coming from private and corporate donations.

The National Liberty Memorial

Opening date: 2009
Location: Washington, D.C., Constitution Garden Lake on the National Mall between the Lincoln Memorial and the Washington Monument
www.libertyfunddc.org

The National Liberty Memorial will honor slaves, freedmen, freedwomen, and others who helped them as they fought for the liberation of the colonies during the Revolutionary War.

The idea for the memorial has been under development since the 1980s. The monument will include a freestanding statue of a Revolutionary War–era black man, woman, and child prepared to fight for their freedom and for the colonies' independence. Surrounding the statue will be a bronze story wall telling the stories of the five thousand African-American soldiers and sailors who were encamped with Gen. George Washington at Valley Forge and fought as members of the American army at Yorktown, Monmouth, and other major Revolutionary War battles. The memorial will sit near the center of the National Mall on the shores of the lake in Constitution Gardens, directly across the lake from the 56 Signers of the Declaration of Independence Memorial.

The spot where the National Liberty Memorial will be located was the original location of the Black Revolutionary War Patriots Memorial, which was authorized by Congress to be one of the last monuments built on the National Mall. In 1988 lawmakers approved the site at Constitution Gardens between the Lincoln Memorial and the Washington Monument because a memorial to African-American Revolutionary War patriots qualified as being of "preeminent historical and lasting significance to the nation." However, after years of fundraising, the supporters of the effort were unable to raise enough money to bring their project to fruition, and the authority to build on the site expired in 2005.

Supporters of the National Liberty Memorial—some of whom were the founders and original supporters of the Black Patriots Memorial—are now trying to get Congress to substitute their proposal for the failed first attempt. Senators Christopher Dodd (D-CT) and Charles Grassley (R-IA) introduced legislation in 2006 to preserve the land on the National Mall for the National Liberty Memorial. Until that legislation is approved, the National Mall Liberty Fund D.C. is not taking donations for the construction of the monument.

The Benjamin Banneker Memorial

Opening date: Expected around 2010
Location: Washington, D.C., the L'Enfant Plaza Promenade
www.bannekermemorial.org
202-387-3380
Donations can be sent to:
Washington Interdependence Council
2020 Pennsylvania Avenue NW
Suite 225
Washington, D.C. 20006

Benjamin Banneker is best known for his work in helping to survey and design the nation's capital. He served as assistant to the geographer general who was initially hired to survey the area that became the District of Columbia. The nation's capital named Banneker Overlook Park (near L'Enfant Plaza and only steps away from the Smithsonian Institution museums) in honor of Banneker's work.

His supporters now want to erect the Banneker Memorial, which also will be built along the L'Enfant Plaza corridor. Preliminary plans for this memorial include a fourteen-foot statue of Banneker, a Founding Architect's Visitors Center, a forty-foot tower clock, and exhibits surrounded by a lush, new park setting.

Former president Bill Clinton lauded Banneker as "this Nation's first African-American man of science." "It is appropriate to honor this great American by erecting a memorial here in the District of Columbia, where Mr. Banneker employed his celebrated talents to survey and establish the boundaries of the Federal City," Clinton said in 1998 as he signed legislation to establish the new memorial.

The Washington Interdependence Council—sponsors of the memorial—unveiled several different possible designs for the Banneker Memorial in November 2006, the two-hundredth anniversary of Banneker's death. A competition will be held to select the final design.

Selected Bibliography

Books

Aikman, Lonnelle. *We, the People; The Story of the United States Capitol, Its Past and Its Promise,* 3rd ed. Washington, D.C.: United States Capitol Historical Society, 1965.

Alexandria Convention & Visitors Association. *A Remarkable and Courageous Journey: A Guide to Alexandria's African American History.*

Allen, William C. *The Dome of the United States Capitol: An Architectural History.* Washington, D.C.: U.S. Government Printing Office, 1992.

———. *History of the United States Capitol: A Chronicle of Design, Construction, and Politics / Prepared under the Direction of the Architect of the Capitol.* Washington, D.C.: U.S. Government Printing Office, 2001.

The American Story in Art: The Murals of Allyn Cox in the U.S. Capitol. Washington, D.C.: National Society of the Daughters of the American Revolution and United States Capitol Historical Society, 1986.

Apdita, Tingba. *The Hidden History of Washington, D.C.: A Guide for Black Folks.* Second in a series. Washington, D.C.: The Reclamation Project, 2004.

Arlington Convention and Visitors Service, Arlington Chamber of Commerce and the Black Heritage Museum of Arlington. *African American History in Arlington, Virginia: A Guide to the Historic Sites of a Long and Proud Heritage.*

Arnebeck, Bob. *Through a Fiery Trial: Building Washington 1790–1800.* Lanham, MD: Madison Books, 1991.

Bancroft, Frederic. *Slave Trading in the Old South.* New York: Frederick Ungar Publishing Co., 1959.

Blassingame, John W., ed. *Slave Testimony, Two Centuries of Letters, Speeches, Interviews, and Autobiographies.* Baton Rouge and London: Louisiana State University Press, 1977.

Click, Patricia C. *Time Full of Trial: The Roanoke Island Freedmen's Colony, 1862–1867.* Chapel Hill: University of North Carolina Press, 2000.

Conner, Jane Hollenbeck. *Birthstone of the White House and Capitol*. Virginia Beach, Va.: Donning Co., 2005.

Douglass, Frederick. *Narrative of the Life of Frederick Douglass, an American Slave, Written by Himself.* Edited by Benjamin Quarles. Cambridge, Mass.: Belknap Press, 1960.

Drayton, Daniel. *Personal Memoir of Daniel Drayton, for Four Years and Four Months a Prisoner (for Charity's Sake) in Washington Jail.* Boston: B. Marsh; New York: American and Foreign Anti-Slavery Society, 1855.

Eberlein, Harold Donaldson. *Historic Houses of George-Town & Washington City*. Richmond: Dietz Press, 1958.

Eliot, William G. *The Story of Archer Alexander: From Slavery to Freedom, March 30, 1863*. Boston: Cupples, Upham & Co., 1885.

Executive Committee of the American Anti-Slavery Committee. *Slavery and the International Slave Trade in the United States of America*. Anti-Slavery Collection. London: Thomas Ward & Co., 1841.

Federal Writers' Project. *Washington, City and Capital*. Washington, D.C.: American Guide Series, 1937.

Fitzpatrick, Sandra, and Maria R. Goodwin. *The Guide to Black Washington: Places and Events of Historical and Cultural Significance in the Nation's Capital*. New York: Hippocrene Books Inc., 2001.

Gates, Henry Louis, and Cornel West. *The African-American Century: How Black Americans Have Shaped Our Country*. New York: Free Press, 2000.

Gilbert, Olive. *Narrative of Sojourner Truth: A Bondswoman of Olden Time, with a History of Her Labors and Correspondence Drawn from Her Book of Life*. New York: Penguin Books, 1998.

Green, Constance Mclaughlin. *The Secret City: A History of Race Relations in the Nation's Capital*. Princeton: Princeton University Press, 1967.

Keckley, Elizabeth. *Behind the Scenes: Formerly a Slave, but More Recently Modiste, and a Friend to Mrs. Lincoln, or, Thirty Years a Slave and Four Years in the White House*. Edited by Frances Smith Foster. Urbana: University of Illinois Press, 2001.

Kennon, Donald R., and Richard Striner. *Washington Past and Present: A Guide to the Nation's Capital.* Washington, D.C.: United States Capitol Historical Society, 1987.

Kennon, Donald R., ed. *The United States Capitol: Designing and Decorating a National Icon.* Athens: Published for the United States Capitol Historical Society by Ohio University Press, 2000.

Latty, Yvonne, and Ron Tarver. *We Were There: Voice of African American Veterans, from World War II to the War in Iraq.* New York: Amistad, 2004.

Lomax ,Virginia. *The Old Capitol and Its Inmates.* New York: E. J. Hale & Son, 1867.

Mitchell, Alexander D., IV. *Washington, D.C., Then and Now.* San Diego, Calif.: Thunder Bay Press, 2000.

Moore, Christopher. *Fighting for America: Black Soldiers—The Unsung Heroes of World War II.* New York: Presidio Press, 2005.

Nalty, Bernard C. *The Right to Fight: African-American Marines in World War II.* History and Museums Division, Headquarters, U.S. Marine Corps, 1995.

Pacheco, Josephine F. *The Pearl: A Failed Slave Escape on the Potomac.* Chapel Hill: University of North Carolina Press, 2005.

Seale, William. *The Presidents' House, Vol. 1.* Washington, D.C.: White House Historical Association with the cooperation of the National Geographic Society, 1986.

Simmons, Rev. William J. *Men of Mark: Eminent, Progressive and Rising.* Cleveland, Ohio: Geo. M. Rewell & Co., 1887.

Smith, Jessie Carney, ed. *Black Firsts: 2,000 Years of Extraordinary Achievement.* Detroit, Mich.: Gale Research, 1994.

Smith, Steven D., and James A. Zeidler. "A Historic Context for the African American Military Experience." Champaign, Illinois US Army Corps of Engineers, Construction Engineering Research Laboratories, 1998.

Smithsonian Anacostia Museum and Center for African American History and Culture. *The Black Washingtonians: The Anacostia Museum Illustrated Chronology.* Hoboken: J. Wiley, 2005.

Smithsonian Institution. *African and African American Resources at The Smithsonian.* Washington, D.C., 1996.

Tuckerman, Henry Theodore. *Book of the Artists; American Artist Life Comprising Biographical and Critical Sketches of American Artists, Preceded by an Historical Account of the Rise & Progress of Art in America,* 2nd ed. New York: J. F. Carr, 1867.

Washington, D.C., Convention and Visitors Center. *Washington, D.C., African American Historical Attraction Guide.*

Wiencek, Henry. *An Imperfect God: George Washington, His Slaves, and the Creation of America.* New York: Farrar, Straus and Giroux, 2003.

Articles

The Alexandria Gazette, August 21, 1939.

Allen, William C. "Capitol Construction—United States Capitol Building; African American Construction Labor." *American Visions,* February–March 1995.

———. "History of Slave Laborers in the Construction of the U.S. Capitol." June 1, 2005. Unpublished Congressional report.

Byrne, Karen. "We Have a Claim on This Estate: Remembering Slavery at Arlington House." *Cultural Resource Management Online,* no. 4 (2002).

Charleston Daily Courier, September 11, 1862.

Chase, Henry. "Memorable Meetings: Classic White House Encounters—Presidential Meetings with African American Leaders." *American Visions,* February–March 1995.

Heard, Sandra R. "Presenting Race and Slavery at Historic Sites: Manassas National Battlefield Park; A Cooperative Research Project between the National Park Service and the Center for the Study of Public Culture and Public History of the George Washington University." February 6, 2006.

"Indiana's Black Regiment: Black Soldiers for the Union." *The Indiana Historian,* Indiana Historical Bureau, State of Indiana, February 1994.

Jacobs, Harriet. "Life among the Contrabands." *The Liberator,* September 1862.

Kapsch, Robert J. "Building Liberty's Capital: Black Labor and the New Federal City." *American Visions,* February–March 1995.

Kirk, Elise K. "Black Performers at the White House: A Picture History." *American Visions,* February–March 1995.

Kurin, Richard. "In the Service of the Presidency—African Americans on the White House Domestic Staff." *American Visions,* February–March 1995.

"Man of Mark, Solomon G. Brown." *The Smithsonian Associates Civil War E-Mail Newsletter* 7, no. 4.

New York Tribune, December 10, 1863.

Painter, John H. "The Fugitives of the Pearl." *Journal of Negro History* 1 (June 1916).

Petersburg Daily Express, April 1, 1865.

Schreiber, Susan P. "Interpreting Slavery at National Trust Sites: A Case Study in Addressing Difficult Topics." *Cultural Resource Management* 23, no. 5 (2000).

Seale, William. "The Untold Story of Blacks in the White House." *American Visions,* February–March 1995.

———. "Upstairs and Downstairs: The 19th-Century White House—African Americans." *American Visions,* February–March 1995.

St. Louis Daily Times, January 2, 1876.

The Washington Star, May 30, 1862.

Walton, Eugene. "Philip Reid and the Statue of Freedom." *Social Education* 69, no. 5 (September 2005).

Wennersten, John R. "A Capital Waterfront: Maritime Washington, D.C., 1790–1880." Unpublished manuscript. Available online at http://www.nmhf .org/pdf/capital_waterfront.pdf.

Wilkins, Sharron E. "The President's Kitchen—African American Cooks in the White House." *American Visions,* February–March 1995.

Internet Resources

African American Heritage Database. "Cultural Tourism D.C." www.cultural tourismdc.org/info-url3948/info-url.htm.

The African American Registry official Web site. www.aaregistry.com/.

Architect of the Capitol. "The Statue of Freedom." www.aoc.gov/cc/art/
freedom.cfm.

Arnebeck, Bob. "The Use of Slaves to Build the Capitol and White House
1791–1801." www.geocities.com/Bobarnebeck/slaves.html.

Becker, Eddie. "Chronology on the History of Slavery and Racism 1790–1829."
www.Innercity.Org/Holt/Chron_1790_1829.Html.

Bendiner, Erin Michaela. "African Americans in Capitol Artwork: A Glimpse of
American History." *The United States Capitol Historical Society History &
Exhibits: Featured Historical Articles.* www.uschs.org/04_history/subs_articles/
04e_05.html.

Congressional Medal of Honor Society. "William Carney, the Flag Bearer."
www.cmohs.org/recipients/carney_history.htm.

National Park Service. "African American Seamen." www.nps.gov/archive/
pevi/HTML/afro-amer.html.

———. "Interpretation at Civil War Sites: A Report to Congress, March 2000."
www.cr.nps.gov/history/online_books/icws/Index.htm.

National Parks Conservation Association. "Analoston Island on the Potomac and
the First District Colored Volunteers Regiment." www.npca.org/
cultural_diversity/treasures/analostan.html.

Senate Historical Office. "1878–1920: February 14, 1879. Former Slave Presides
Over Senate." www.senate.gov/artandhistory/history/minute/
Former_Slave_Presides_Over_Senate.htm.

———. "Blanche Kelso Bruce." www.senate.gov/artandhistory/art/artifact/
Painting_32_00039.htm.

Ushistory.org Independence Hall Association. "Enslaved Africans in the President's House." www.ushistory.org/presidentshouse/slaves/index.htm.

The White House Historical Association. "A Colored Man's Reminiscences of
James Madison by Paul Jennings." www.whitehousehistory.org/08/subs/
08_B01.html.

About the Author

Jesse J. Holland is a nationally recognized journalist and media personality from Washington, D.C., who for years has combined his work as a political writer for the world's largest news organization, The Associated Press, with a love of African-American history and news.

In addition to being responsible for coverage of the confirmation process of the three most recent Supreme Court justice candidates—Justices John Roberts and Samuel Alito, as well as failed nominee Harriet Miers—Holland has written hundreds of stories about African-American politics, history, and news for the *New York Times* and for The Associated Press in Washington; Columbia, South Carolina; and Albany, New York.

In 2004 Holland became the first African American ever elected to the Congressional Standing Committee of Correspondents, a congressionally created committee

PHOTO BY VICKI KELLIEBREW

of journalists elected by their Washington, D.C., peers to represent the Congressional Press Corps in front of the Senate and the House of Representatives.

Holland has been a guest on a number of shows discussing African-American and Washington political topics; he has appeared on C-SPAN's *Washington Journal*, ABC's *News Now*, and WHUT-TV's *Evening Exchange with Kojo Nnamdi*.

He is also the former host of *The Wednesday Agenda* radio talk show on WUMS-FM in Oxford, Mississippi, and has appeared as a guest on the *Inside Albany* political television show in Albany, New York, and WIS-TV's *Newswatch* in Columbia, South Carolina.

Holland is a member of the prestigious National Press Club, the National Association of Black Journalists, and the Washington Association of Black Journalists, and he is one of the creators of the former newspaper comic strip "Hippie and the Black Guy." He is also a co-founder of two National Association of Black Journalists chapters: the University of Mississippi Association of Black Journalists and the South Carolina Midlands Association of Black Journalists. He is an active member of the Washington Press Club Foundation, which promotes and provides funding for aspiring female and minority journalists.

Originally from Holly Springs, Mississippi, Holland graduated from the University of Mississippi with degrees in journalism and English. While at Ole Miss, he was only the second African-American editor of the daily campus newspaper, *The Daily Mississippian*. He now lives in the historically African-American section of Washington, D.C.'s, Capitol Hill neighborhood with his wife, Carol, and his daughter, Rita.